INDIAN FRONTIER WARFARE

INDIAN FRONTIER WARFARE

G. J. YOUNGHUSBAND

GYAN

Published by

Gyan Publishing House
5, Ansari Road
Daryaganj, New Delhi-110002
Phone: 011-47034999, 9811692060
E-mail: books@gyanbooks.com

Distribution Network
gyanbooks.com
India, USA, Canada, UK, Australia

ISBN: 978-93-6780-198-7 (PB)

First Published, 1898

2nd Impression 2024

Printed at: Gyan Press, Delhi.

INDIAN FRONTIER WARFARE
Author: G. J. YOUNGHUSBAND

INDIAN FRONTIER WARFARE.

INDIAN FRONTIER WARFARE.

BY

CAPTAIN AND BREVET-MAJOR

G. J. YOUNGHUSBAND, P.S.C.,

ASSISTANT-QUARTERMASTER-GENERAL,

AUTHOR OF

"*The Queen's Commission*," "*Frays and Forays*,"
"*The Relief of Chitral*," *etc., etc.*

FORMING THE THIRD VOLUME

OF

The Wolseley Series

EDITED BY

CAPT. WALTER H. JAMES.

LONDON:

KEGAN PAUL, TRENCH, TRÜBNER & CO., LTD.,

PATERNOSTER HOUSE, CHARING CROSS ROAD.

1898.

Gibraltar, April 19th, 1897.

DEAR CAPTAIN JAMES,

I HAVE read with interest the list you have sent me of the military works to be published as "The Wolseley Series."

The subjects are wisely chosen, and the authors will be generally accepted as soldiers who are competent to express valuable opinions upon them.

I am much flattered by having my name associated with an undertaking that is designed to improve the professional knowledge of our officers, and I rejoice to feel that under your able editorship its success is assured. In some instances I see you are not only editor but also translator, for which duty, if you will allow me to say so, your intimate knowledge of the German idiom eminently qualifies you.

I hope the officers of her Majesty's army may never degenerate into bookworms. There is happily at present no tendency in that direction, for I am glad to say that this generation is as fond of danger, adventure, and all manly out-of-door sports as its forefathers were. At the same time, all now recognize that the officer who has not studied war as an applied science, and who is ignorant of modern military history, is of little use beyond the rank of Captain. The principle of selection, pure and simple, is gradually being applied to the promotion of all officers, especially in the higher grades. As years go on this system will be more and more rigidly enforced.

It is gratifying to know that a large proportion of our young officers are ambitious, and without doubt there is now many a subaltern who hopes to be a Field-Marshal or to be shot in the attempt. Experience enables me to warn all these determined men of how small their chance is of ever reaching any great position in the army unless they devote many of their spare hours every week to a close study of tactics and strategy as dealt with in the best books upon recent wars.

In this series of military works from the pens of first-class writers, the military student will find ample material to assist him in fitting himself for high command, and in the interest of the Empire and of the army I earnestly hope he will avail himself of it.

I know how truly this work is undertaken as a labour of love by you as editor and by all who are helping you. But I also know that you and they will feel amply repaid if it assists the young officer to learn the science of his profession and, in doing this, to improve the fighting value of the service, to the true interests of which we are one and all sincerely devoted.

Believe me to be,

Very truly yours,

WOLSELEY.

TABLE OF CONTENTS.

LIST OF MAPS.

LIST OF INDIAN TERMS WITH THEIR ENGLISH EQUIVALENTS.

Atta	=	Flour.
Dacoit	=	An armed robber.
Dhal	=	A kind of pulse.
Dandy	=	A species of open sack slung on a pole in which a person can be conveyed.
Dhooly	=	A palankin or palkee of light construction in which wounded are carried.
Duffadar	=	Native Sergeant.
Jemadar	=	Native Lieutenant.
Kôtal	=	A mountain ridge.
Kote-Duffadar	=	Troop Sergeant-Major.
Lance-Duffadar	=	Lance-Sergeant.
Naik	=	Native Corporal.
Puggri	=	A turban, the Native head-dress.
Sangar	=	A stone breastwork.
Salutri	=	Native Veterinary Assistant.
Sowar	=	Trooper.
Subadar (Infantry), Ressaidar (Cavalry), Ressaldar (Cavalry)	=	Native Captain.
Subadar-Major (Infantry), Ressaldar-Major (Cavalry)	=	Senior Native Officer in the Regiment.
Syce	=	A Native groom.
Wurdi-Major (Cavalry)	=	Native Adjutant.

INDIAN FRONTIER WARFARE.

CHAPTER I.

GEOGRAPHICAL, TACTICAL, AND GENERAL.

The land frontiers of India extend in one great sweep from the Mekong River and the territories of the King of Siam in the far east, along the vast extent of mountain ranges known generally under the title of the Himalayas, to the spurs of the Hindu Kush, the inhospitable Afghan hills, and the deserts of Beluchistan. On every tribe and clan, on every pass and trade route along this immense extent of frontier, the Indian Army has to keep its steadfast watch and ward. Scarce a mile of this frontier but holds an open or secret foe; scarce a year passes without the necessity arising of armed intervention in one quarter or another. For against the solid wall of British rule the sea of outer barbarism beats ever restlessly.

Though the broad strategical principles on which civilized warfare is based throughout the world are the same, yet local conditions so far alter their tactical bearings that methods suitable to the country and the foes to be encountered have had to be gradually evolved in the course of practice. Thus in India the experience gained during decades of constantly recurring frontier expeditions has taught the Indian Army how to modify the broad principles which obtain in Europe to agree with local conditions. To give some brief record of the methods employed in Indian Frontier Warfare is the object of this book.

Anyone with a map of India in his mind's eye, will easily appreciate that, in passing along so vast a frontier, we must encounter tribes whose characteristics and methods of waging warfare are entirely different; we must pass through countries and districts in which the physical features vary greatly, and we must be prepared to find the rocky mountains of one part replaced by the mighty forests or swampy jungles of another. Thus, commencing from the Indian Ocean and passing round the frontier eastward, we come upon the Beluchis, the Waziris, the Afghans, the Afridis, Swat and Chitral, the Black Mountain tribes, Nepaul, Thibet, Bhootan, the Chins, Lushais, and Shans, besides many other smaller and less important tribes and countries. We have the great forests of Burmah and the Shan States, the densely jungled hills of Sikkim and Bhootan, the bare rocky fastness of Chitral and Afghanistan, and the arid deserts of Beluchistan. In any one and every one of these regions, and against each and all of these tribes, does the Indian Army find itself in conflict from time to time.

Not only in physical features and tribal characteristics does one part of the frontier differ widely from another, but on a continent where such immense distances intervene between different parts of it, it is only natural to find great climatic variations. Intense cold, with snow and ice, in one part may be contrasted with a close, moist, malarious heat in another; and whilst on one portion of the frontier the fierce power of the sun makes marching by day almost impossible, on another the rain may be pouring in cataracts at the rate of six inches a day.

We have stated above that the broad principles of strategy and tactics are the same all over the world, but perhaps it would be wise here to particularize more freely. A great military writer has defined strategy as "common sense," and tactics as "common sense." If this be so, then Indian strategy and Indian tactics are one and the same thing as European strategy and European tactics, and the *raison d'être* of this treatise disappears. But the military student will require a more extensive view and will not rest content with an epigram. Thus the first step we take, beyond the broad one of "common sense," at once leads us into vastly different results issuing from the same definition.

To take a few instances which come readily to hand. No general with any pretence to strategical or tactical skill would in European warfare and against a civilized foe deliberately divide his forces in the face of an enemy of superior numbers. He would eschew wide turning movements; he would avoid, if possible, fighting a battle parallel to his communications, much less facing his proper rear; he would not make a practice of attacking vastly superior numbers in strong positions with inferior numbers. He would, in fact, show his common sense, his strategical and tactical knowledge in studiously avoiding those very movements and very manœuvres which, in Indian warfare, have won us some of our most brilliant victories. Having said so much it may seem that victory in India lies in throwing all first principles to the winds. This is not the case. It will be found as we get deeper into the subject that these great victories and great campaigns have not been won by a brutal disregard of all the traditions of regular warfare, but by a nicely-balanced discrimination which enabled the leader to so gauge the capacity of his enemy as to make movements, hazardous against another foe, not only safe, but by their very boldness conducing more to safety than would a strict adherence to the ordinary rules of warfare. In Asiatic warfare it has become an axiom sanctified by time, and justified by a hundred victories, for a British force, however small, always to take upon itself the rôle of the attacking party. From the battle of Plassey downwards this bold initiative has almost invariably brought success. In Europe, or against a European foe met under similar circumstances, to attack would in many cases be tactically unsound, and in some positively disastrous. Indeed it will be noticed that, whether compelled by inferiority in numbers or from other causes, the British Army in Europe has won most of its most celebrated battles by employing what are termed defensive-offensive tactics. That is by receiving the enemy's attack in a selected and perhaps prepared position, and when he has exhausted his efforts in vain assaults, to issue comparatively fresh and unshaken, and to hurl him fiercely into the abyss of defeat. The battle of Waterloo will readily occur to the reader as a typical case in point.

On the other hand the enemies we have to meet in Asia undoubtedly invite attack. With the exception of the Waziris, and occasionally the Afghans, the Asiatic, however great his numbers, prefers fighting on the defensive in a prepared position. Now although he and his forefathers have been fighting against us, on and off, for a couple of centuries, and though his positions are often chosen with the greatest skill, yet, curiously enough, he almost invariably leaves open a loophole for flank attacks or turning movements. Moreover, having on such occasions watched his British opponents disintegrating their forces in the execution of wide turning movements, he has never yet trained his forces to be sufficiently disciplined or sufficiently mobile to take advantage of this favourable circumstance by delivering a counter attack.

In fighting against some of the less stout-hearted tribes on the frontier it is indeed often sufficient to make merely a show of cutting them off from their communications to at once cause an evacuation of the strongest positions. Yet it must be remembered that communications, in their proper sense, are not to such an enemy what they are to us. His army has no regular base, no commissariat, no transport. Each warrior carries his food, his kit such as it is, and his ammunition on his person, and when he is defeated makes the best of his way to his own home, and sets to work tilling his field. On the other hand, though his skill does not lie in winning battles, yet he excels in that most useful form of operation, the harassing of the enemy's communications. Thus it will be found, as on the Khyber line in the last Afghan war, that to keep open and safe, in the face of an enemy thus skilful, the communications of a fighting force of say 10,000 men, every mile of its lines of communication would require about one hundred men.

In Europe the theatre of war is usually intersected by great roads, metalled for the passage of guns and carts. Rivers are bridged at all important points. Railways facilitate concentration and the carriage of supplies; whilst important towns and large villages are dotted over the auntry, affording food and shelter to the troops. On the frontiers of India it is far otherwise. Here mere goat tracks, hardly passable for pack transport, take the place of roads. Rivers and mountain torrents are unbridged, or at best spanned by frail foot-bridges. Railways often do not exist within several hundred miles of the point of attack. The countries which are the scene of operations are generally so wild, so miserably poor, so destitute, as to afford neither food nor shelter for the troops, nor forage for the animals. Lastly all operations in a tropical country, where arid wastes and stony mountains replace the richly-cultivated and well-watered hills and valleys of Europe, are rigidly bound down by considerations of water.

The immense difficulties that have to be overcome

in the matter of supply and transport are very aptly illustrated by the operations which were undertaken for the relief of Chitral in 1895. The force employed at the commencement of the campaign was 15,000 men, afterwards augmented to 18,000. When the leading brigade reached Chitral the force was distributed along some 170 miles of country, and it required 28,000 pack animals, and later, when the local crops were consumed, 38,000 pack animals, to keep this force supplied with its daily bread, ammunition, and stores. When we consider that those 38,000 animals had themselves to be fed, guarded, and cared for, we shall in some degree appreciate the fact that the defeat of the enemy in battle is by no means the most difficult task put before the leader of an Indian frontier expedition.

For many years after British territory had expanded to its present frontiers, it became customary, probably owing to the paucity of troops available, and the difficulty and danger of concentrating them at one point, thereby leaving another unguarded, to meet raid by raid—in other words, to employ only small parties of local troops for striking rapid blows at vulnerable points in return for blows received, and after inflicting as much loss as possible, to return again to our own territory. As communications improved and railways crept up closer to the frontier these punitive raids gave place to organized expeditions on a more extended scale. It was found more effective if more expensive to thoroughly master the enemies' country and dictate terms at leisure in their midst. The experience thus gained has been of undoubted value to the Indian Army, and more especially to the senior combatant and departmental officers. On the other hand, young officers, non-commissioned officers, and men do not, under the changed aspect of affairs, have the same advantage of gaining the splendid training in self-reliance, boldness, and responsibility which independent command gives. Nevertheless the days for young officers on the frontiers are not altogether past as was most heroically illustrated by the wars in Burmah during 1885-86-87. During the second period of this prolonged campaign, whilst Sir George White was in command, no less than one hundred separate and distinct engagements with the enemy took place, and in the vast majority of these young officers were acting alone, on their own responsibility, as sensible units of the great combined operation for the pacification of Burmah.

Other brilliant feats of arms, such as the defence of Thobal by Lieut. Grant with a handful of men, mostly recruits, and the defence of Chitral fort, a seemingly untenable position, against vastly superior forces, live nobly in the history of the Indian Army. Many others not less heroic lie well-nigh forgotten amidst the dusty leaves of some official report.

We must also not forget, in treating of Indian frontier warfare, to take into consideration the great question of the health of the troops. Soldiers, both British and Native, have often to campaign in regions where the climate is to one or other and sometimes to both so different to the usual conditions under which they are accustomed to live as to come under the designation of deadly. As long as active operations are going on and the excitement of battle is upon them, the troops keep in splendid health. But long months, perhaps years, of constant and harassing work by night and day, the escorting of convoys, and even the mere idleness of living in a fixed camp, bring sickness and death amongst the troops. In Afghanistan during the two years which the campaign lasted, from November, 1878, to the autumn of 1880, the total losses in killed, wounded, and invalided was 50,000; or a number approximately equivalent to the entire force that was in the field at any one time. Of this number the very large majority were invalided, or died of disease. During what was known as the "death march" from Gundamuk to Peshawur, at the end of the 1879 campaign, one battalion was so decimated and reduced by cholera that it practically ceased to be a fighting force, and the survivors reached the base a mere collection of sick conveyed in carts. In Burmah, with its damp malarious heat, the troops were, in some regions, invalided by hundreds, and whole regiments had to be drafted elsewhere. It stands to reason then that not only must the arrangements for supply and transport be perfect, but the organization of the medical department must be such as to stand the immense strain that is sometimes thrown upon it. The Military Surgeon has not to contend with the overwhelmingly concentrated work which a great battle between two European Powers gives to one of his profession, but he has an equally formidable task in contending against the deadly diseases which campaigning in a tropical climate almost invariably beget.

Thus, though it is customary in dealing with military subjects to give the place of honour to the sieges, battles, and combats of a campaign, the fact must not be lost sight of that battles cannot be fought and won without food for man and beast; and that more lives are lost from sickness and disease than are sacrificed on the battlefield. The veteran Marshal Saxe gave to the world the celebrated phrase, "The secret of victory lies in the legs." Though not so neat it would be even more true, and especially so in an Indian frontier war, to alter the phrase by one word and make it, "The secret of victory lies in the stomach." For one thought which a commander will give to the enemy before him he will give a dozen anxious thoughts to the supply and transport of his force. He fully grasps the fact that to leave his men one single day without food is more lowering to their *moral* than would be a check before the enemy; and that an army which has been starved for a week may be in a worse condition than it would after a severe defeat. There is nothing heroic about the commissariat, there is nothing glorious about the transport, but brilliant victories and desperate defeats not infrequently owe their origin to these less imposing but vitally important and integral portions of modern campaign organisation.

Following then the general custom, we will first deal with combats and fighting, and later describe more in detail the working of those great departments which form the machinery of war.

CHAPTER II.

Mountain Warfare.

The art of war is at all times difficult, but perhaps mountain warfare affords some of the most intricate problems in that difficult art. Deserts and forests each enhance the complexity of ordinary warfare, but a campaign in the mountains not only affords its own special difficulties, but in addition sometimes those of the desert and of the forest. Not only have immense physical difficulties to be overcome, but the veriest desert affords as much support to an army as does the inhospitable mountain region which may form the theatre of operations. Thick forests in the plain country have their dangers and difficulties, but these are enhanced a hundredfold when not mountains alone or forests alone have to be dealt with, but a combination of the two in forest-covered hills. It will perhaps be convenient for the better examination of the subject if we deal with each class of warfare separately, starting first with warfare in barren mountains such as are to be found on the northern and western frontiers and in Afghanistan; next proceeding to deal with campaigns in forest-covered countries, such as Burmah, where considerable rivers also play a part; and finally refer to expeditions into those densely-wooded hill tracts which are to be found on the North-Eastern frontiers.

Further the operations suitable to each theatre will be described both under their offensive and defensive aspects. To commence then with the rugged warfare of the North-West frontier.

In civilized war one of the chief endeavours of the commander of an invading force is to conceal as long as possible the actual point of invasion. He will use every endeavour to leave the enemy in doubt up to the last moment as to his intentions; by this device hoping to commit him to such a dispersion of his force as the guarding of all approaches would necessarily involve. Such a device is rarely necessary, or rarely resorted to, in Indian frontier warfare, though an exception may be quoted in the case of the Chitral campaign. Here, at the opening of the campaign, access to the Swat Valley was possible by three passes, each held by the enemy in about equal strength. Sir Robert Low's first intention was to make a simultaneous attack in force on two of these passes whilst a demonstration was made against the third; but at the last moment he changed his plans, and, concentrating rapidly to his left, stormed one pass with his whole force whilst demonstrations only were made against the other two. In this instance, time was a matter of the greatest importance, and all unnecessary fighting was to be avoided, but as a general rule it is very far from a general's wishes or intentions to conceal his point of attack, for this reason, that usually the great difficulty is to induce the astute mountaineer to enter upon a regular pitch battle. Each belligerent very naturally endeavours to meet the other on ground most favourable to himself. Thus a highly-trained, admirably organized and equipped force will use its best endeavours to bring about a set battle, in which its superior training will give it the advantage. On the other hand, bands of guerillas without training, and with little organization, will, wherever possible, avoid a regular battle, and will instead endeavour to meet their opponents with all the arts and devices of partisan warfare, that being the class of war in which their peculiar skill gives them a decided advantage.

It is in this endeavour to bring mountaineers to the test of actual battle that so many of those wide turning movements which would be fatal to success in European warfare have their origin. Experience has shown that in the majority of cases to make a frontal attack, or even a combined frontal and flank attack, has indeed the effect of driving off and dispersing the enemy, but with little or no loss; and he is ready at a moment's notice to collect again in force, uninjured and unshaken. If the capture of an important strategical point be alone the object of the attacking force, then if this be attained, no matter how, the desired end is gained. But when, as is generally the case, the decisive defeat of the enemy's troops, and not only the capture of a position, is the object of the attackers, the result is not so satisfactory.

The opening of the Afghan War in 1878 gave two very useful instances of the effect of wide turning movements, and though in neither case did events turn out quite as anticipated by the commanders, yet the main result was in each case satisfactorily attained.

The first was afforded by the turning movements which resulted in the capture of Fort Ali-Musjid, which bars the entrance to the Khyber Pass. The plan of operations consisted of a frontal attack by one brigade, a simultaneous flank attack by a second brigade, which, however, had to make a wide detour through the mountains before it could reach its position, whilst a third brigade made a wide turning movement, also through the mountains, on to the enemy's rear. Imperial policy directed that the attack should take place on a certain day and almost at a certain hour, with the result that Sir Sam Browne, who was in command, was committed to an isolated frontal attack with one brigade, whilst the flanking brigade did not arrive in time to come into action at all, and the turning brigade, owing to the difficulty of the country, did not reach its post till from 12 to 24 hours after the allotted time. The nature of the country did not allow of inter-communication between brigades or with divisional headquarters. The operation was therefore a somewhat risky one, and would not, of course, in face of a European enemy have been attempted. As it happened the frontal attack was repulsed by the Afghans, who held a position practically impregnable to direct assault; but during the course of the night following the battle the effect of the pressure of the turning brigade, which was now astride of the enemy's line of retreat, made itself felt, with the result that the Afghans evacuated the Ali-Musjid position. In this case not only was the capture of an important point attempted, but also the capture of the enemy's forces.

The Battle at the Peiwar Kotal, which took place a few days after on a different line of advance, was another instance of a wide turning movement. And in this connection it may be well to point out that a wide turning movement does not necessarily mean one which passes through a large arc of country, but one which, owing to the physical features of the intervening country and natural obstacles, such as mountains, rivers, swamps, or forests, is cut off from direct communication with the remainder of the force.

In the case of the Peiwar Kotal the main body of the force executed the turning movement, whilst a comparatively small force was left behind to act as a containing force and to demonstrate against the enemy's front. Thus 2,263 men and 8 guns accompanied Sir Frederick Roberts in his turning movement, whilst 1,000 men and 5 guns remained for the frontal attack. The turning movement commenced at 10 p.m. on the night of December 1st, 1878, and it was not till the evening of the next day that the enemy were finally routed. During the greater part of that time, as Sir Frederick Roberts himself thoroughly appreciated, his force was in a most precarious position, for failure on the part of the turning party would have meant the severe defeat if not entire annihilation of the whole force.* Only the gravest necessity would justify so serious a risk as this, and that necessity appears to have existed on this occasion.

* See Lord Roberts' "*Forty-one Years in India.*" Vol. II., p. 135.—Ed.

Repeated and careful reconnaissances had demonstrated that the only way to capture the Peiwar Kotal was by a turning movement of this description, retreat was out of the question, and therefore *faute de mieux*, the only course which held out any promise of success, had to be followed. It is perhaps open to question whether a general, if called upon to fight a battle over again, would invariably do so in exactly the same way, In this case it is open to conjecture whether it would not be decided after the experience gained to diminish the numbers of the turning party and proportionately to strengthen the force left as a containing force to guard the camp, and later make a frontal attack. For apart from the fact that a small force can move much quicker by night than a large one, it will be noticed that, strung out as it necessarily is in such a country along a single file track, a large force cannot be brought to the front at the moment of each successive attack. It would therefore be more useful elsewhere. Further the defeat of a small turning party would not necessarily jeopardise the safety of the whole force.

These two instances very clearly bring out one of the salient points in Asiatic warfare, that as long as troops are boldly led it is possible, after justly calculating all chances, to engage in operations which if judged by European standards would rightly be considered too dangerous. The effect of these two blows was to shatter completely the whole of the regular Afghan army, which did not again take the field from this date to the signing of the treaty of Gundamuk.

CHITRAL EXPEDITION 1895.

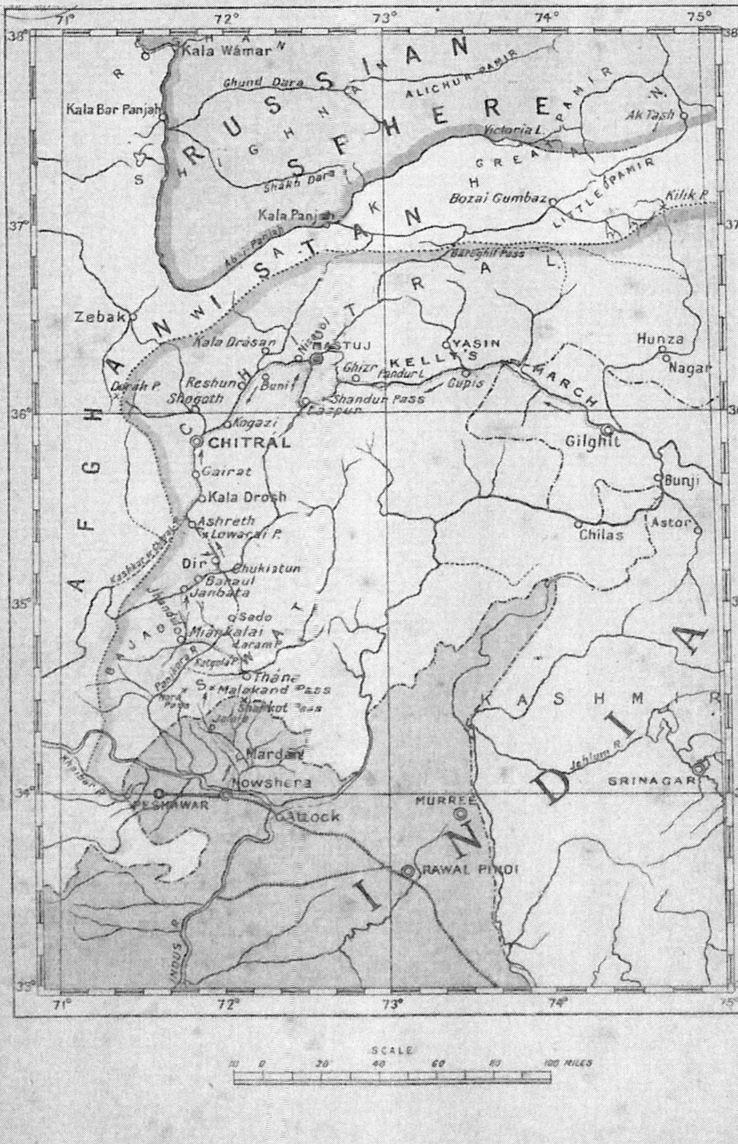

Though after carefully balancing the chances, and with a thorough appreciation of the enemy's characteristics and modes of warfare, dispersed and disconnected attacks are not only allowable, but very generally successful against unorganized troops, yet a strict adherence to first principles will often obtain the same results, though to the uninstructed onlooker the same appearance of brilliancy may be absent.

An instructive instance in point was afforded by a problem which arose during the advance of Sir Robert Low's force to the relief of Chitral. The position to be faced was this: The fort of Chitral was closely beleaguered by immensely superior numbers, and was in danger of falling at any hour. It was therefore of the greatest importance to arrive there as soon as possible. Sir Robert Low with two brigades had arrived on the banks of the Panjkora River, being then about 100 miles from Chitral. The river was then in flood and formed an impassable obstacle for troops until a bridge could be built. Two roads led to Chitral—one up the west bank, on which side lay the British force, the other after making a detour led up the east bank. Fifty miles up stream these two roads met at the bridge of Chukiatun, and henceforth became one as far as Chitral. Umra Khan with 9,000 men lay opposite Sir Robert Low, at the point where he reached the Panjkora River. The question was, would it be wiser to push troops up the west bank, seize the bridge at Chukiatun and push on to Chitral, leaving Umra Khan and his force behind with a brigade to watch them, or to remain concentrated, bridge the river, and fight a decisive battle before pushing on. Both alternatives were feasible, and had it not been for the question of time and the immense importance of arriving rapidly in the vicinity of Chitral the comparative merits of the two plans would hardly require discussion. As it was the question was a very nice one. Between Sado, Sir Robert Low's camp, and the bridge at Chukiatun not only was the river unfordable but ran through rugged mountains, forming a defile quite unsuitable for the rapid movement of mounted men. There was no possibility therefore of seizing the bridge by a sudden dash of cavalry. The bridge itself was a very precarious one, built of logs on the cantilever principle, stretching from cliff to cliff over a roaring torrent, and could easily be demolished by unskilled labour in half an hour. A force therefore going by this road might find its way completely blocked by the destruction of the bridge and the opposite bank held by several thousand men.

Though, as events proved, a small force of infantry and guns would have been successful in seizing the Chukiatun Bridge, which in the most unaccountable manner was left practically unguarded, yet undoubtedly Sir Robert Low chose the safer course in adhering to first principles. He bridged the river at Sado, and crossing over fought a decisive battle with Umra Khan before proceeding further. And here be it observed that though apparently time would have been gained by the more daring but risky dispersion in the presence of superior numbers which the alternative plan entailed, yet, in reality, the gain would have been apparent rather than real. For the decisive defeat of Umra Khan in the Jhandol Valley, 80 miles from Chitral, relieved Chitral as effectively and probably on the same date and hour as the more risky undertaking would have done.

In this connection may be mentioned a *ruse de guerre*, which undoubtedly helped materially towards gaining the desired end Following in the train of Sir Robert Low's force was a local chief, who had some years previously been expelled by a revolutionary party from the country in which the British force was now operating. This chief had a small following of armed men, and could count on being joined by some of his old adherents as soon as they perceived that he was on the crest of an advancing tide of success. When, therefore, it was decided not to send a flying column *en l'air* to Chitral, the presence of this chief afforded an opportunity of producing an almost equal effect. He was therefore dispatched up the west bank of the Panjkora, giving out far and wide that he was merely the advance guard of an overwhelming British force following close at his heels. The effect was excellent. His following grew by hundreds; he seized and crossed the Chukiatun Bridge, pushed a force of ragtag and bobtail over the Lowarai Pass, and his emissaries penetrated up to the very walls of Chitral, giving out far and wide the close approach of the relieving force. This *ruse de guerre*—for the composition and armament of this chief's force could hardly entitle it to be looked upon as a serious military operation—undoubtedly helped materially in the general plan of operations for raising the siege.

As was mentioned above, the enemy's troops and not tactical or strategical points in his country are, as a rule, the objective of an expeditionary force. But failing the enemy's troops, his most important and richest villages are aimed at, and the burden of his misdeeds is brought home to him by the confiscation of his cattle, the destruction of his crops, and the burning of his houses. In undertaking offensive operations against a tribe, it is therefore usual, reversing the policy of earlier years, to do so with the utmost deliberation. The most favourable time of year climatically for our own troops will be selected, and one which will combine the desiderata of finding the enemy's crops standing and his cattle in the valleys. The exact point or points of invasion will be published to all who care to learn them; the exact day and hour of invasion is known to all, friends and foes alike. Such expeditions are not as a rule very interesting, nor do they afford much scope for tactical skill, but they are necessary and at the same time most useful, not only giving administrative experience, but teaching both officers and men, in the most practical manner possible, the rudiments of serious warfare. They supply in fact that element of danger and reality the absence of which makes ordinary peace manœuvres so devoid of interest and often of instruction. The frontiers of India may therefore be described as the training ground of the troops, and as such undoubtedly have no equal in the world.

But the lessons here learnt must, as regards offensive warfare, be intelligently applied rather than blindly taken as precedents. Broad principles should be assimilated and the careful working out of the same made to suit the existing circumstances. Used intelligently the experience which the Indian Army from year to year perforce gains, should place it in a position to meet with confidence the best troops of any nation.

Having said so much on the general subject of offensive warfare let us examine the subject more in detail, taking as examples such operations as may from time to time appear to be the most instructive.

First in importance amongst the mountainous campaigning grounds of the Indian Army must be placed that portion of the frontier which is known generally and collectively under the title of the North-West Frontier. This portion extends from the borders of Kashmir to our outposts at Quetta, and comprises within its limits all the most warlike of those tribes with whom our continental position brings us in contact. From North to South this stretch of country is about 800 miles in length, and may be described as consisting of a mass of bleak and rugged mountains. These mountains vary in height from 3,000 feet to 12,000 feet, and in their midst nestle narrow but not altogether unfertile valleys, in which the warlike inhabitants live, and raise their scanty crops, or feed their flocks and herds.

The British boundary proper may be said to coincide throughout a greater portion of its length with the low foothills which spring from these mountain ranges. The great plains of India are in fact British territory, whilst the great ranges that border those plains are inhabited by semi-independent tribes, between whom and ourselves constant causes of strife arise. These armed contests arise as a rule from a few set causes, and amongst the most frequent may be found disputes about land, the raiding of cattle, wholesale murder, and arson. The origin of the quarrel may be merely an unimportant and purely domestic difference of opinion, between two villages, one being on the British side of the border and the other on the foreign side. From virulent abuse to cattle lifting and counter lifting is but a step; this may necessitate the interference of the police first, and later perhaps of the military. And so from small beginnings formidable combinations may arise, culminating perchance in a small battle. Or it may so be that the members of some recalcitrant tribe through a long series of years have committed murder and other high crimes and misdemeanours within Her Majesty's domains, fleeing from justice to trans-border regions. In such a case formal notice would be sent to the head of the tribe concerned, announcing that unless the outlaws were given up a fine of so many thousand rupees or so many head of cattle would be levied against the tribe. Such an ultimatum is very usually met with a series of prevarications and excuses, the sum total of which amounts to a tacit refusal to accept the terms offered. When consequently a long series of crimes remains unsettled, a further ultimatum is sent to the obdurate tribesmen warning them that if all claims are not settled by a certain date an armed force will enter their country, with a view to exacting substantial damages. Affairs having reached this crisis, diplomacy as often as not fails, and it is found necessary to send an expedition to bring the belligerent tribesmen to reason.

Be the causes, however, of the campaign what they may, the execution of it in a hill country follows as a rule certain well-defined precedents. The punitive force enters the hostile region by one, two, or three routes, and concentrates at the chief centre of the enemy's resistance, usually a clump of fortified villages, situated in the best watered valley. Sometimes there is an initial or final battle, more often not; and the fines having been levied and securities taken for future good behaviour the force returns to its cantonments in India. With such apparent ease and uniform success are these expeditions carried through that it might appear to the uninstructed observer that their execution offers no difficulties. Such a conclusion would be far from correct. With troops less highly experienced in mountain warfare, leaders less skilful, and organization less perfect, we should have had to record many a defeat which now stands on the rolls of the Indian Army as a victory. Accumulated experience, improvement in armament, reorganization of the transport and commissariat departments, have from year to year borne their fruits, with the result that it is gradually being brought home to our hereditary enemies across the border that the old days of equal chances in a campaign have departed, at any rate for a time.

It is contended by some that those who are skilled in mountain warfare are skilled in the most difficult branch of the art of war. Whether this be so or not it is an undoubted fact that campaigns in mountainous countries afford most valuable training not only to the leaders, but to all officers and men.

In Europe the main ranges are for the most part traversed by fine roads, suitable for the passage of artillery and wagons. Not so the mountains on the Indian frontier, where single-file cattle tracks take the place of metalled roads. In these regions thus isolated by the lack of roads are no supplies that can reasonably be counted upon; water is often scarce and far apart; forage is partially or entirely unobtainable. Warfare in such a theatre is, in fact, warfare in a mountainous desert, so deserted indeed in some parts as to be incapable of supplying the smallest wants, even of firewood. It is apparent therefore that, apart from the actual fighting, immense difficulties have to be overcome in connection with the administration of the commissariat and transport services. Further, it must be borne in mind that in face of the warlike inhabitants any hitch in the smooth working of the operations, any unforeseen difficulties or partial failures, place the troops at once at a disadvantage which a brave and ubiquitous foe is not slow to avail himself of. As long as all is going well not an enemy may be seen, but the moment matters go wrong for want of supplies or other reasons, making a retreat or even a cessation of hostilities necessary, it will be found that every rock and boulder holds a concealed enemy, and thousands of armed bandits will appear as if by magic to threaten the flanks and rear of the invaders. It is at such a moment and in warfare of this description that the border warrior shows his greatest skill. To even highly trained and veteran troops a retreat under such circumstances is a most trying ordeal. It is needless therefore to suggest that it is a cause for legitimate endeavour with every general to save his troops from such an ordeal in so far as administrative forethought is capable of securing immunity.

In all countries which may become the possible theatre of operations there is one season of the year more favourable than another for an invading force. In Europe, though campaigns have lasted throughout the twelve months of the year, yet no Power responsible for the declaration of hostilities would willingly commence a campaign till after the rigours of winter were passed. On the same principle it is found that as a rule the most favourable time for commencing an offensive movement on the Indian frontier is in the spring or autumn of the year. For not only is the climate at these seasons more equable, but the small patches of spring or autumn standing crops which are found here and there help the troops to a certain degree, whilst their confiscation is one of the severest blows which the hostile tribesmen can suffer. Intense heat, the rainy season, and intense cold are, whenever possible, avoided.

The student of Indian military history will have been impressed with the striking boldness with which even small and isolated bodies of British troops assume the offensive in battle, and how comparatively small forces boldly take the initiative be the country invaded small or great. This tradition has been worthily carried down to our own times; it is still found both tactically and strategically sound to assume the offensive and to take the initiative. It will therefore perhaps be most appropriate if we commence with offensive movements, and dealing first with the more important operations where comparatively large bodies of troops have been employed, proceed later to give some account of the many gallant feats of arms performed by detachments and small bodies of troops.

BATTLE OF CHARASIA.

October 6, 1879.

The advantage of taking a bold initiative even under apparently very adverse circumstances is very clearly exemplified by the battle of Charasia. Those acquainted with the history of our relations with Afghanistan at this period will remember that in September, 1879, the British Envoy, Sir Louis Cavagnari, and the whole of his escort had, in time of peace, been treacherously murdered by the Afghans at Kabul. Immediate steps were taken to revenge this atrocious breach of international faith, and imperial policy directed that a decisive blow should be struck, with the troops immediately available for the undertaking, rather than risk loss of prestige by the slower though safer medium of an organized and methodically worked out campaign.

It was thus that Sir Frederick Roberts found himself, when within a march of Kabul, confronted by the whole Afghan army, strongly entrenched, his communications with India broken, his baggage and trains cut off, and surrounded on all sides by many thousands of a fiercely hostile and fanatical peasantry.

The British force consisted of 5½ battalions of infantry, 9 squadrons of cavalry, and 18 guns, the total strength of the force being 3,800 men, including gunners,* but of these only 2,650 men were available to take part in the battle. The enemy's position lay along a chain of heights through which three roads led to Kabul. Of these the road along which the British had intended advancing follows the course of the Logar River, which here bursts through, the range forming a defile named Sang-i-Nawishta. At daybreak an advance guard consisting of a wing of the 92nd Highlanders and the 23rd Pioneers had been sent forward to seize this defile, but the Afghans were already in possession, and before the advance guard could reach the defile the enemy's troops could be seen in large numbers and regular formation crowning the crest line of the hills. His position extended from the Sang-i-Nawishta defile, both sides of which

* Lieutenant-Colonel W. S. Lockhart in *Gazetteer of Afghanistan*, article "Chárásiá."

were strongly held, on his extreme left, to the heights above the Chardeh Valley, which formed his right, a distance of about three miles. The general form of the defensive position was that of an arc, facing south. The portion of the position most strongly held was the ridge to the west of the Sang-i-Nawishta gorge, which varied in height from 1,000 feet to 2,000 feet above the plain, and a strong outpost was placed on a semi-detached hill which covered the entrance to the gorge. Twelve guns were placed in position on the west of the gorge, and four Armstrongs in front of the hill. Along the front of the whole position lay sandy barren undulating hills, forming easily defensible bastions to the main line of defence. At the foot of these inferior heights was a bare stony slope descending to the arable land round Charasia and the hamlet of Khairabad. The main position commanded the whole ground in front, and was inaccessible except at a few points.

Sir Frederick Roberts' original intention had been, as we have seen, to seize the Sang-i-Nawishta defile, but the enemy, rightly gauging his intentions, had so strongly garrisoned it as to make the undertaking both hazardous and costly. The General therefore changed his dispositions, and, using his original advance guard as a containing force to face and menace the Sang-i-Nawishta defile, he made preparations for attacking the enemy's less strongly held flank, away to the west. Leaving therefore 700 Infantry and 450 Cavalry to protect his camp and to watch the hostile combinations of freebooters who hovered round on every side, Sir Frederick Roberts detailed 2,000 men, under Brigadier-General T. Baker, to undertake the difficult task of attacking and driving in the enemy's right flank. Moving to the left of Charasia Village and covered in some measure by its outlying walled enclosures, this force emerged at 11.30 a.m. into the open, and immediately became engaged with a large number of the inhabitants of the neighbouring villages, supported by a considerable force of regular troops. Working steadily forward and obliquely across the front of the enemy, General Baker at length seized with a company of the 72nd Highlanders a small peak beyond the extreme right flank of the enemy's position. This right flank was in itself an exceedingly formidable obstacle, consisting of a peak 2,000 feet high, practically inaccessible in front, and very difficult of ascent at any other point, whilst the fire from it swept the slopes up which the attacking troops must advance. The company of the 72nd Highlanders, which had secured the flank position above mentioned, could make no further progress, and was reinforced by two companies of the 5th Gurkhas, whilst to give this flanking force a helping hand the remainder of the 72nd Highlanders and two guns of the mountain battery made a demonstration in the form of a frontal attack. The peak at this point was, as before mentioned, practically inaccessible, and no material progress was made. The enemy, now fully aware that the real attack was being made on their right flank instead of on the Sang-i-Nawishta defile, began to transfer troops rapidly to reinforce the threatened point. General Baker had already seven battalions of regular troops besides hosts of irregulars to contend against, and therefore rightly judged that he must push his attack home before the enemy's reinforcements arrived. Sending forward therefore 200 men of the 5th Punjab Infantry and two companies of the 5th Gurkhas to strengthen the frontal attack, whilst the 23rd Pioneers acted as a support, he pushed forward, and, after two hours' hard fighting, gained a footing on the ridge somewhat to the eastward of the flanking peak, and partially piercing the enemy's centre. The result of this success was that the defenders of the peak came under a heavy cross fire and were compelled to evacuate it, taking up, however, a second position 600 yards in rear. Forming up again for attack, General Baker placed the 72nd Highlanders, two companies of the 5th Gurkhas, and two companies of the 23rd Pioneers in the front line, and supported them with the remainder of the 23rd Pioneers and the detachment of the 5th Punjab Infantry. Covered by the fire of the mountain guns, the line advanced by alternate rushes, and after half an hour's fighting captured the second position.

In the meantime the small containing force, under Major G. S. White, 92nd Highlanders, placed opposite the Sang-i-Nawishta defile, had, when its opportunity came, taken the offensive and had engaged the Afghan left with great success. Allusion has been made to a small semi-detached hill which covered the mouth of the defile; this was at about 12.30 p.m. stormed by two companies of the 92nd Highlanders, and the three field guns were at once pushed forward, and fromthis point engaged the enemy's four advanced guns, which were apparently supported by three battalions of Infantry.

As soon as it became apparent that General Baker's primary attack had proved successful, Major White detached two companies of the 92nd Highlanders, who from the direction of their attack materially assisted General Baker in driving the enemy out of his second position. The enemy's right flank and centre was now completely shattered, but he still clung tenaciously to the Sang-i-Nawishta defile. Turning inward, therefore, General Baker swept along the ridge, and Major White, seizing his opportunity with alacrity, stormed the defile in brilliant style and drove out the enemy, capturing the whole of his artillery. The defile being now gained, the small body of cavalry with Major White, consisting of detachments of the 9th Lancers and the 5th Punjab Cavalry, dashed through in pursuit, supported by a detachment of the 92nd Highlanders, and materially assisted in routing the enemy.

We have here a very notable example of a commander extricating himself from a well-nigh untenable position, forced on him by considerations outside those which usually guide the conduct of a campaign, and not only extricating himself from it, but at the same time wresting a decisive victory from the enemy. The astonishing boldness of the tactics employed will be of especial interest to the European student as emphasizing once more the apparent liberties that can be taken by a bold and experienced leader in dealing with an enemy whose *moral* and methods of war he is sagacious enough to gauge. Sir Frederick Roberts' total force consisted of 3,800; of these 1,150 had to be left behind to protect the camp, leaving only 2,650 men to deal with the enemy. The enemy's position was three miles long. In dealing with a modern European enemy, it has become an accepted axiom that it is most dangerous to make a flank march in the immediate vicinity and within striking distance of the enemy. But the Afghan Army of that period was far behind European models in discipline, mobility, and tactical experience. It was indeed in no more advanced a condition than were the enemies whom the Prussians had to meet in the days of Frederick the Great. History has made us familiar with the stereotyped form of battle of that era. The enemy was drawn up and possibly entrenched along some well-defined feature of ground. The Prussians were formed up and facing it, in two or three lines. Frederick then gave the order "troops and companies right wheel;" marched serenely round to a flank; gave the order to wheel into line and forthwith attacked. And so immobile was the enemy, and so incapable even of reinforcing threatened portions within its own line, that these tactics were almost invariably successful. The tactics employed at Charasia against an equally uneducated enemy were exactly those of Frederick the Great. The whole force, with the exception of a small containing force, marched boldly to a flank, overwhelmed it, and rolled the enemy's line up from right to left. It will occur to the military student to ask why the Afghan commander, seeing the British force committed irrevocably to an attack on his extreme right, did not boldly issue, with irresistible numbers, from the Sang-i-Nawishta defile, brush aside the small containing force, swamp the camp and its guard, and with his force augmented by the thousands of free-lances hovering around, descend like a torrent on the already much embarrassed ammunition and commissariat trains under MacPherson some miles in rear. The result of such a counter attack might have resulted in the entire annihilation of the British force.

Though experience of its methods has taught us that the Afghan Army was not at that period mobile enough to take advantage of the varying tactical conditions of a battle, yet it would not be safe to take it for granted that such will necessarily be the case in the future. As the enemies of Frederick the Great learnt in the bitter school of defeat how to meet and overcome his manœuvres, so we must calculate, as the years go on, on educating our enemies in the same manner up to a higher level of tactical skill. As they improve in armament and improve in discipline, so proportionately will the problems alter which a British commander will have to solve.*

In European or indeed Asiatic warfare, it is naturally advisable to concentrate one's forces before entering on a decisive engagement. But occasionally circumstances outside the pale of purely tactical or strategical considerations force the hand of a commander and compel him to undergo risks to which he

* The losses suffered in the recent operations (October, 1897) would seem to bear out the truth of this prophecy.—Ed.

would not willingly expose himself. Thus before giving battle at Charasia, Sir Frederick Roberts would undoubtedly have first cleared away the enemy who obstructed the road between himself and his trains a few miles in the rear, and drawing in MacPherson and his rear guard, would have parked his ammunition and stores in the camp, and then with a free hand and strengthened by a couple of extra regiments have commenced the battle. But there was no time to effect this, for it was imperatively necessary that the enemy should be dislodged from his strong position before dark. His occupation of the heights barring the road to Kabul was a menace that could not be brooked—a warning that could not be disregarded. Behind these heights lay the densely crowded city of Kabul, surrounded by villages and hamlets swarming with armed men, each and all of which had sent their contingents to aid the defenders. And it did not require much experience of Afghans and their ways of thought to appreciate the fact that, if left in undisturbed possession of the heights for the night, the morning would find their force augmented by many thousands. Therefore, though the British by delay might have been strengthened by MacPherson's two regiments, the enemy would in the same period have received considerably larger additions to their strength in numbers, besides being allowed further leisure to fortify and strengthen their position.

SAMANA.

Amongst the best-known and most successful of modern frontier leaders may be mentioned the name of General Sir William Lockhart. This officer's long experience in India, and in the many frontier wars, including the Bhootan Campaign, the Black Mountain Expedition, the Afghan War, the Burmese Expedition in 1886-7, in command of the two Miranzai Expeditions in 1891, the Isazai Expedition in 1892, and the Waziristan force in 1894-5, in addition to his experience in Abyssinia and with the Dutch in the Acheen Expedition in 1875-7, show a record which few can equal in this particular kind of warfare. The methods of such a leader cannot fail to be instructive and to afford useful precedents in the execution of future operations on the frontier.

RE-TAKING OF THE SAMANA RANGE.

In March, 1891, the Samana range, which lies about 40 miles east of Kohat, had been newly occupied by our troops, small posts being garrisoned to hold the crest and to protect the working parties employed on improving the communications. Partly by treachery and partly by surprise, these posts were captured by the enemy on April 4th, and their garrisons were driven down into the plains with heavy loss.

Orders were immediately issued for the concentration of a force consisting of ten Infantry regiments, six squadrons of Cavalry, three batteries of Mountain Artillery, and one company of Sappers and Miners, to re-capture the Samana range; the operations being entrusted to Sir William Lockhart. The Samana range is a ridge of heights, some sixteen miles in length, running generally east and west. The various peaks along its course vary from 4,440 feet to 6,550 feet in height. On the south side, running parallel with the range, and distant from it from two to four miles as the crow flies, lies the Kohat-Hangu-Darband-Baliamin road, along which the troops for the attack were distributed. On the north side, and also running more or less parallel to the range, is the Khanki River. At its eastern end the range inclines gradually to the Khanki Valley, and at its western extremity dips sharply into the Gharu Valley. The whole range is very rugged and rocky, with a few trees and scrubs scattered here and there, and water is very scarce.

The enemy held generally the crest of the range with their advanced troops, numbering 1,000, whilst the main body was in rear in the Khanki Valley. The dispositions made for the attack were as follows:

The force was divided into three columns. Of these the first column, consisting of four battalions of Infantry, one mountain battery, and half a company of Sappers and Miners, was at Hangu.

The second column, consisting of three battalions of Infantry, one mountain battery, and half a company of Sappers and Miners, was at Darband.

The third column, consisting of three battalions of Infantry and three mountain battery guns, was also at Darband.

The general plan of attack was for the first column to scale the range near its eastern extremity and then, turning westward, to sweep along its entire length. Meanwhile the second and third columns, moving from Darband and Pat Darband, situated respectively 4½ and

$8\frac{1}{2}$ miles west of Hangu, were each in succession to attack the range, each to its proper front, waiting, however, till the first column, moving from its flank position, was so placed as to be able to effectually co-operate with it. The operation may, in fact, be described as a series of combined frontal and flank attacks, whilst to cut off all chance of the enemy escaping by way of the Khanki Valley, six squadrons of Cavalry were held in readiness to sweep round the eastern spurs of the range.

In accordance with these plans, the first column moved off from Hangu at 6 a.m., and covered by the guns, reached the summit of the ridge without serious opposition at 8.30 a.m. This column having now successfully gained its flank position, orders were heliographed to the second column, distant about four miles, to attack that portion of the range which lay opposite it. The combined operation then commenced, but the enemy, threatened in flank and attacked in front, gave way and streamed off westward, whilst the two attacking columns effected their junction without loss. Sending the second column down into the far valley, and ordering it to move parallel with him, Sir William Lockhart continued his advance along the ridge with the first column. Meanwhile the third column was in its turn put in motion, and the same manœuvre was repeated. On this occasion, however, the enemy made a stand at the fortified post of Tsalai, which, at 12.30 p.m., was assaulted by the Infantry of the first column, covered by the fire of artillery. Gogra and Sangar were next carried by the first column, and at 2 p.m. a junction was effected with the third column, which, after some fighting, had pushed up the hill, driving all before it.

It will be noticed that the tactics employed placed the enemy in an extremely awkward position. At each point where he had determined to make a stand he was assailed simultaneously in front and on his flank, whilst in the valley to his rear sat six squadrons of Cavalry. An organized army, or a force less agile on the mountain side than these hardy mountaineers, would infallibly have been slaughtered to a man or taken prisoners if the battle had gone against them. But as it was, though their loss in men was heavy, and in prestige, the bread of life to the Afghan or Pathan, enormous, they managed to effect a very creditable retreat. This was effected not by dropping down into the valley to their rear, but by working off to the westward, along the side of the rear face of the range. As will be noticed in other examples given, the great difficulty in mountain warfare against guerillas, as these Afghan tribes may fairly be called, is to bring them to book. They have no lines of communication in a proper sense, no base, no commissariat, no transport. They can disperse and collect with astonishing rapidity, and that not only by recognized routes, but by mountain paths known only to a few local people. Attacked in front, flank and rear, and heavily defeated though they may be, yet the majority generally manage to escape by some loophole, scattering for the time being, but living to fight another day. In this connection it may not be inappropriate to draw attention to the fact that it is by no means always the endeavour of the General to completely surround the enemy. Most of our campaigns on the frontier have to be fought against heavy odds in the matter of numbers; and these mountaineers, if caught absolutely without an opening for retreat, are capable of fighting with such desperation that the weight of numbers must tell, and the necessary dispersion of the attacking force lays it open to a severe reverse. Such a reverse occurred at Chilas, and will be described in its proper place. It is therefore more usual, and safer and sounder tactically, unless the attacking force is so strong that each of its columns is alone equal to dealing with the enemy, so to attack the enemy that the main object of the battle may be gained without running the risk of suffering such a reverse as would be possible from driving him to desperation.

During this battle we have a good instance of the value of the heliograph as a means for transmitting orders whilst operations are actually in progress. It will be noticed that immediately the first column reached its flank position a heliographic message was flashed down to the second column, 4½ miles distant as the crow flies, to move forward to the attack. To have sent a message round by an orderly would probably have occupied a couple of hours. At the same time it must be remembered, and especially so in fighting a European foe, that messages thus flashed might be read by the enemy, who being thereby let into the secrets of the opposing force makes his dispositions with his eyes open to frustrate them. Hitherto the ignorance and backwardness of the border tribes has made the use of the heliograph perfectly safe, and as in the above case most valuable, but undoubtedly if we in any future campaign have to meet the Amir of Afghanistan's regular troops, some caution in its use will be necessary. On the other hand it will in that case be open to an astute general, finding his messages are read and understood by the enemy, to signal false orders and false dispositions, thereby perchance deceiving the enemy and at the same time sufficiently concealing his own designs.

Since Lord Roberts made his famous march from Kabul to Kandahar the Indian Army has perhaps taken part in no campaign so rapid, brilliant, and successful as the operations which resulted in the elief of the garrison of Chitral in the spring of 1895. No element was wanting to call forth the keenest instincts of the soldier, or to arouse the anxious interest of those who watched with breathless suspense the keen struggle, as the columns pushed forward over high mountain passes, girth deep in snow, across rivers broad and deep, swollen with rain and melting snow, and fiercely opposed by the desperate bravery of mountain warriors born and bred to the sword.

Before the opening of the campaign our knowledge of that portion of the theatre of operations which lies between the Peshawur Valley and Chitral territory was limited almost entirely to such information as had been collated from the reports of natives. This information, though defective in accuracy of detail, yet described with sufficient exactness the main physical difficulties to be overcome. Speaking generally, the theatre of war was crossed transversely by ranges of high mountains and rapid rivers, each in itself a formidable obstacle, culminating in the lofty range through which a pass 10,450 feet high alone gave access to Chitral. Of the country which lies between Chilas and Chitral, by the route followed by Colonel Kelly's column, we had accurate knowledge, the route having been frequently traversed by troops and an accurate survey made. The stupendous task before Colonel Kelly, moving at this time of year (March—April) could therefore be fairly gauged beforehand.

With the fuller knowledge we now possess it is possible to give more in detail the physical features of the country through which the Relief column from Peshawur passed. Skirting the broad open plain in which Peshawur is situated is a range of mountains varying from 3,000 feet to 6,000 feet in height and known locally and collectively as the "border hills," for, generally speaking, the British border runs along the foot of this range. Beyond the border range lies the richly cultivated Swat Valley, varying in width from two miles to three miles, and having an extent of some thirty-six miles lengthways. Down this valley flows the Swat River, a considerable stream at all times of the year, but after the snows begin to melt, and the summer rains burst, a large and rapid river. Some estimate of the size of the river may be gained by noting that at the point first bridged by our troops, it is about half a mile wide from bank to bank, being split up into seven channels, each requiring a separate bridge. The north side of the Swat Valley is formed by the Laram range of mountains, varying from 5,000 feet to 6,000 feet in height. Beyond this range we come to the southern extremity of the Principality of Dir, down the main valley of which flows the formidable and treacherous Panjkora River. This river which one day is fordable may the next be found a roaring torrent, many feet deep; indeed on one occasion it rose fourteen feet within a few hours, with little or no warning. The Panjkora Valley throughout its length is narrow, with steep rocky spurs constantly running down to the water's edge, and except in the depth of winter, when the water is at its lowest, was not suitable, without extensive road making, for the passage of troops.

Lying to the north-east of the Panjkora Valley, and separated from it by high ranges, we find the broad, open, fertile valleys of Jhandol and Bajaur, the former of these being the original home and limited territory of the chief Umra Khan, against whose power the British expedition was mainly directed. Skirting the north end of the Jhandol Valley comes the Janbata range, varying from 6,000 feet to 10,000 feet in height, crossing which we drop into a series of narrow rocky valleys, which betoken the approaches to some great mountain range. Such are the Baraul and upper Dir Valleys, with no room for cultivation on any scale and barely capable of supporting a miserably poor and backward race. Running transversely across the north corner of Dir territory we find the mighty range of mountains, from 10,000 feet to 20,000 feet in height, over which the Lowarai Pass alone gives military access to the Chitral Valley. The Chitral Valley is itself very narrow and rocky, much on a par with the Panjkora Valley, and was, till a track was cut, very difficult for the passage of troops.

Briefly it may be stated that four high ranges of mountains, and three considerable rivers, besides mountain torrents, had to be crossed by the Southern column of the Relief Force.

The country through which the small Northern column under Colonel Kelly had to pass was still more rough and rugged. Moreover he was practically isolated, and had to depend entirely on his own resources for those necessaries which are requisite for pushing an armed force through a difficult country under the most unfavourable climatic conditions. The highest pass which was crossed by this column was over 12,000 feet.

Speaking generally then, the theatre of war may be described as a mass of mountains, amidst which wind deep and rapid torrents, whilst here and there may be found small open valleys with sufficient supplies only to maintain the inhabitants.

The plan of operations for the Relief of Chitral consisted of a combined movement from north and south, the Southern column, 15,000 strong, being considered capable of holding its own against any combination that might arise, whilst the Northern column consisted of 400 men, lightly equipped, whose errand it was to arrive as soon as possible, and by the moral effect of their arrival more than by actual force of arms to prolong the siege sufficiently for the arrival of the main relief force. The Southern force was based on Nowshera (near Peshawur), whilst the Northern column was based on Gilghit.

The enemy's main base of operations was Jandul, the home of the ruling spirit in the camp of the besiegers of Chitral. Hence Umra Khan drew the pick of his men, his treasure lay here, and from it he obtained such arms and ammunition as he possessed. If we look at Jhandol on the map and examine its relative position to Chitral and Peshawur we shall at once see that a decisive blow struck from the direction of Peshawur must inevitably jeopardise Umra Khan's base of operations, with the probable result that he would be compelled to leave Chitral and retreat hastily to defend his own country. The Peshawur column in fact by the nature of its march must take him directly in rear, and he must either abandon his own country to the invader in the hope of first striking a decisive blow at Chitral, afterwards turning on his tracks to meet Sir Robert Low, or else he must perforce abandon the siege and concentrate his forces to meet the British before they could gain a footing in his territory. The relative position of the belligerents being thus, it is apparent that the first objective of the main column of the relief force was Jhandol. But though at first sight the advantage of position lay with the British, yet one important item entered into the problem which made the balance even, and that was the consideration of time. It was calculated that the Chitral garrison was only provisioned up to the end of April, and therefore to effect its relief a decisive blow must be struck before that date. Such a possibility

Umra Khan and his lieutenant Sher Afzul were inclined to discount. An organised army moves slowly, immense physical difficulties stood in its way, and the inveterate animosity of 30,000 tribesmen could infallibly be counted upon. In a matter which depended upon days and even hours there was a distinct advantage on the side of the besiegers.

This being the first occasion on which a serious mobilisation of any part of the army had been attempted, the experiment was watched with much interest by military critics. It must be remembered that to mobilise a force on the Indian frontier is a far more complicated and difficult problem than to mobilise a force at Metz or Strasburg. In Europe many railways lead to important points of concentration, the distances are comparatively short, and countries which are likely to become the theatre of war are intersected by numerous railways as well as roads suitable for heavy wheeled traffic. Large towns and flourishing villages are to be found at the end of every march, and the country invaded is capable of supplying to a very great extent the wants of the invaders in the matter of commissariat and transport. Far differently situated is a force on the Indian frontier destined to penetrate into the inhospitable mountains which frown along its whole length from the Bay of Bengal to the deserts of Beluchistan. For such a force, the whole of the supplies for the men and followers, as well as nearly all the grain, and much even of the hay, for the animals, has to be carried up to the most advanced troops from the base in India, and carried not along macadamised roads in capacious carts, but by mountain paths where pack transport is alone possible.

There is a popular error that the impedimenta of an Indian Division is enormous. As a matter of fact during the active part of this campaign the allowance per man for everything was from 10 to 15 lbs., and per officer 40 lbs., and no tents were allowed. When we consider that an ordinary soldier's blanket weighs 4 or 5 lbs., an allowance of 10 lbs. need not be considered extravagant in a country where snow and ice, heavy rain, and the fiery heat of the sun had in turns to be encountered. Yet marching thus light 28,000 pack animals had to be collected to feed and maintain the force. It will be apparent then that the problem of mobilisation on the Indian frontier is very materially complicated by the there existing conditions. Not only have the troops and their stores to be concentrated, but also many thousands of pack animals, and the supplies for the entire force, man and beast, for as long as the campaign lasts, have to be collected. Add that in this case units had in some instances to come immense distances, that the line of railway was a single one, and that the detraining station was a small roadside station without platforms or conveniences for disembarking troops, animals, and stores, and we have a series of difficulties which would try severely the most perfectly organized scheme of mobilisation.

It must be a source of gratification to the Indian military authorities that the scheme and the railway stood the severe test applied to them. On the twelfth day of concentration the Southern Division, fully equipped and provisioned, made the first march of the campaign.

The fort of Chitral, the objective of the campaign, lay about 200 miles from Peshawur and about 220 miles from Gilghit. On March 23rd and 24th, Colonel Kelly's small force started from Gilghit, and on the 1st of April the Southern column made the first march of the campaign. Colonel Kelly's first advance was happily unopposed, and by April 5th he had covered ninety miles and had crossed with his guns the formidable Shandur Pass, standing 12,500 feet in height and then deep in snow. The Southern column had, on April 3rd, stormed the Malakand Pass, and was now in possession of the Swat Valley. Brushing aside a half-hearted attempt to bar his way, Colonel Kelly, on April 9th, raised the siege of Mastuj and marched into that place. He was now within about 60 miles of Chitral. The Southern force fought on April 5th an action at Khar, on April 7th forced the passage of the Swat River, inflicting heavy loss on the enemy, and on April 11th reached the Panjkora River. On April 13th Colonel Kelly pushed on from Mastuj and heavily defeated 1,500 of the enemy placed to bar his way. On the same date a flying force of 1,000 of the Khan of Dir's men under that chief was dispatched towards Chitral. On April 17th, both Colonel Kelly from the North and the Khan of Dir from the South had arrived in the near vicinity of Chitral, and on the same date Sir Robert Low with the main body of the Southern Force met and defeated Umra Khan in a decisive battle. On April 18th the siege of

Chitral was raised, and the sorely pressed garrison relieved.

This short and sharp campaign was a fine example of a combined operation which worked out with singular accuracy. It will be noticed that the two forces employed started from widely divergent bases, that there was no intercommunication, and that one of them was working through a practically unknown country. The military critic will perhaps condemn the use of so small a column as that commanded by Colonel Kelly, taking into consideration the time of year and the great physical difficulties to be overcome. As events proved there is little doubt that the operations of the Southern column, working as it did on sound principles, would have effected the relief of Chitral on the very same day and at the same hour even if the Northern force had never left Gilghit. But it must be remembered that not only had Chitral to be relieved, but also Mastuj, and moreover it was most necessary for a military demonstration to be made in the northern valleys to counteract the effect of the series of disasters which had recently befallen the British cause in those regions. Therefore, though the dispatch of a weak and isolated column may not have been strictly in accordance with first principles, yet the special circumstances of the case made a temporary departure imperative. The effect caused by Colonel Kelly's move was undoubtedly great, not only in reinstating British supremacy amongst those wild mountaineers, but in demonstrating the fact that mountain chains hitherto deemed impassable in winter could be crossed by determined troops.

CHAPTER III.

Forest Warfare.

There is probably no form of warfare which tries more highly the attributes of the individual soldier than fighting in forests, thick bush, or high-grass jungle. The routes through such districts are, as a rule, merely single-file tracts, which meander from village to village, the view is strictly limited, whilst every tree and bush, or clump of grass, may hold a concealed enemy, armed with a rifle and ready to open fire at a range of perhaps only twenty yards. Pitfalls, sharp spikes, and entanglements cumber the way, and each man feels like a solitary being in a vast solitude bristling with dangers. The men to his right and left are scarcely in view, and as he pushes on, perhaps not even quite sure of his direction, often amidst a dead silence, in itself discouraging, the soldier may be excused for appreciating the danger of the task allotted to him. But difficult and dangerous as the work is to the individual soldier, his superior officers have a far more trying and responsible task. To manœuvre even small bodies of troops in the face of a concealed enemy, to be able to steer them to an unseen objective along tortuous paths, to calculate time and space so as to fulfil the obligations of simultaneous attacks from different quarters, all these require the highest form of skill, determination, and boldness on the part of a commander.

The *casus belli*, on the forest-covered frontiers of the east and north-east, is, in so far as the British forces are concerned, as a rule, very much the same as on the rugged frontiers of the west and north-west. The murder of a stray officer, the raiding of a tea garden, interference with rights of trade, or encroachments of frontier are amongst the causes which may bring the affairs of a district to a crisis, and necessitate a recourse to arms.

The objective of the punitive force, on such occasions, and in such a country, will very generally be those coigns of vantage which are afforded by the most important and richest of the enemy's villages. Large gatherings of men, and fighting on a broad front, are not of general occurrence; therefore, important engagements in which large numbers are engaged on either side are the exceptions rather than the rule. The usual *modus operandi* will be a warfare of ambuscades and counter ambuscades, rapid night marches, surprises at dawn, sudden attacks on village strongholds, and systematic confiscation of crops, cattle, and arms.

In a campaign commencing as did the last Burmah War, the first objective was Mandalay, the capital of the country, for this city was to Burmah what Paris is to France—the heart and soul of the nation. The Burmans had an exaggerated notion of their own powers and of the invincibility of their king. An easy-going, pleasure-loving people, who were glad enough to take their lord's assurance that the English were a poor race, chiefly composed of peddlers, who could easily be defeated by magic spells, let alone shot and shell. Mandalay was captured with ease and despatch by

Sir Harry Prendergast, the king deported, and the country annexed. It was then that the troops began to gain their experience of forest warfare. The cause of trouble was not that the placid Burman had the smallest objection to a change of masters, but the temporary suspension of civil administration which came between the deportation of the king and the assumption of power by the British, let loose on the land large bands of bandits and criminals, who, under the cloak of patriotism, attempted to profit by the temporary disorder. The second objective therefore, and one which occupied several years, was the hunting down of these bands of dacoits, as they were called, and the establishment of a settled form of government.

It not infrequently happens that suzerain states situated on our borders, and owing allegiance to the Empress of India, are, by intrigue or carelessness, led to enter into diplomatic relations with foreign and possibly unfriendly states, to the detriment of the common interests which should bind them to their suzerain power. Such temporary departures from the strict path of allegiance call occasionally for the presence of British troops, and the drastic re-establishment of British influence. Such, indeed, was the objective of the expedition against the Sikhim chief, whose territories lie on the borders of Thibet, in the spring of 1888. Regardless of treaties, this chief tacitly shook off his allegiance to the Government of India, and openly and flagrantly placed himself under the protection of the Thibetan Lhama and the Chinese representative in Lhasa.

Again, savage outbreaks, sometimes the work of a few desperadoes and sometimes the result of an organized rising, result in the murder of British officials and the massacre of small detachments. Such incidents must be counted amongst the ordinary risks that must be calculated upon on the borders of a great and expanding empire. Nevertheless instant notice has to be taken of all such outrages and immediate steps taken for the punishment of the offenders, to the discouragement of similar incidents in that state and in those which neighbour it. Such was the origin of the Lushai expedition of 1889, a young officer, Lieutenant J. F. Stewart, of the Leinster Regiment, and two of his men, being attacked and killed whilst employed on surveying duty. The cause of the outrage was a curious and typical one. The perpetrator, a powerful chief, who had no cause of enmity against the British, or against this particular party, attacked and killed them, so as to be able to present their heads as a ransom for his wife, who was in the hands of a neighbouring chief. The objective of a punitive force in such a case is naturally that laid down by the Mosaic law, a head for a head.

Such extensions of empire as occurred when Burmah came under British dominion necessitate, as an inevitable concomitant, the opening up of routes connecting it with neighbouring outlying portions of the Empire, the tangible imposition of British influence on petty tribes, and the accurate survey of portions of country hitherto unmapped. With such objects was the Chin-Lushai Expedition of 1890 organized. The force was intended, firstly, to punitively visit certain tribes that had raided and committed depredations in British territory. Secondly, to subjugate tribes as yet neutral, but by force of circumstances recently brought within the sphere of British dominion. And, thirdly, to explore and open out the country lying between India proper and Burmah.

The atrocious murder of Mr. Quinton, the British delegate, and a large party of officers, at Manipur, in 1891, furnishes another example of the causes that lead up to the despatch of an armed force, the objective in such a case being the punishment of the offenders and the exaction of a just retribution.

Such generally are the causes which are responsible for a call to arms on the Indian land frontiers. The operations of the punitive forces in these regions give us the subject-matter for this chapter, the account of warfare carried on in forests, some dense, others sparse, some mountainous or hilly, others level.

As mentioned before, the actual capture of the Burmese capital, the deposition of the king, and the assumption of sovereignty by the British were accomplished expeditiously and effectively by using the great highway afforded by the Irrawaddy River. It was during the second and prolonged period during which the gradual and systematic pacification of the country was undertaken that the problems afforded by warfare in great forests had to be faced by the British troops and British commanders.

Before descending to details we will first investigate the broad principles acted upon in the pacification of an empire larger than France, covered almost throughout its length and breadth by huge forests, and held by ubiquitous and almost countless numbers of small hordes of bandits. This great operation was entrusted to Sir George White, and we cannot do better than study the method in which the work was accomplished, dealing first with larger issues, and then continuing with a detailed account of the various methods in which the numerous small columns, mostly commanded by very junior officers, fought their small battles, and helped in working out each in his small way the great result.

It is, perhaps, a trite saying that there is nothing new in warfare, that Alexander and Cæsar, Hannibal and Napoleon, each were merely masterly exponents of well-known expedients; but it is perhaps sufficiently apparent that however well we may be read in past history, it is only the commander of genius who grasps the application to a case in hand and uses his knowledge with telling results. Thus, probably, except amongst well-read military students, the pacification of La Vendée by the youthful general Hoche is but an obscure operation, the details of which are entirely forgotten. Yet the problem set before Hoche for the pacification of La Vendée was almost identical with that which had to be faced by our troops in the pacification of Burmah, with this one and greatly increasing difficulty, that the area of Burmah is many times greater than that of La Vendée. It was due to the military genius of Sir Frederick Roberts that Hoche's great work was taken as the basis of the plan of campaign opened in 1886. As an operation of this nature may again fall to the lot of the Indian Army, we make no apology for giving in full the methods of General Hoche, before showing how they were applied in Burmah.

Vendée is a maritime department of France, with an area of 2,588 square miles; surface, flat in the north and west, marshy towards the south; elsewhere undulating and much wooded.—(Johnston.)

The "Bocage" and "Marais," in which operations were carried out, constitute a singular country. The Bocage, an unequal, undulating soil, intersected by ravines, and crossed by a multitude of hedges, which serve to fence in each field, and which have, on this account, obtained for the country the name of the *Bocage*.

As you approach the sea the ground declines till it terminates in salt marshes, and is everywhere cut up by a multitude of small canals, which render access almost impossible. This is what is called the *Marais*. The only abundant produce of the country is pasturage; consequently cattle are plentiful. The peasants only grow corn enough for their own consumption. It contained few large towns. Between the two high-roads extended a track 30 leagues in breadth, where there were none but cross-roads, leading to villages and hamlets. The country was divided into a great number of small farms.—(Thiers.)

General Hoche's object was to completely stamp out rebellion in the insurgent province of La Vendée.

This young general, a skilful politician as well as

soldier,* clearly perceived that it was not by arms that he must endeavour to conquer an enemy with whom it was impossible to grapple, and who was nowhere to be come at; heavily armed soldiers, who were unacquainted with the country, could not equal in speed peasants carrying nothing but their muskets, who were sure of finding provisions everywhere, and were acquainted with every ravine and every copse. He formed a plan which, being followed up with firmness and perseverance, could not fail to restore peace to those desolated districts.

The inhabitant of La Vendée was at once peasant and soldier. Amid the horrors of civil war he had not ceased to cultivate his fields and to attend to his cattle. His musket was at his side, hid beneath straw or in the ground. At the first signal of his chiefs, he hastened to them, attacked the Republicans, then stole away through the woods, returned to his field, and again concealed his piece, and the Republicans found but an unarmed peasant, in whom they could not by any means recognise a soldier. In this manner the Vendéans fought, subsisted, and continued to be almost inaccessible. While they still

* Young Hoche was in every way qualified for the important but difficult duty with which he was charged—the pacification of La Vendée. Endowed by nature with a clear judgment and intrepid character, and an unconquerable resolution, firm, sagacious, and humane, he was eminently fitted for that mixture of gentleness and resolution which is necessary to heal the wounds and subdue the passions of civil war. This rare combination of civil and military qualities might have rendered him a formidable rival of Napoleon, and possibly endangered the public peace, had he not united to these shining parts a patriotic heart and a love of liberty, which rendered him superior to all temptation, and more likely to have followed the example of Washington than the footsteps of Cæsar or Cromwell.—(Alison).

possessed the means of annoyance and of recruiting themselves, the Republican armies, whom a ruined administration could no longer support, were in want of everything, and found themselves in a state of utter destitution.

The Vendéans could not be made to feel the war except by devastation, a course which had been tried during the time of Terror, but which had only excited furious resentments without putting an end to the civil war.

Hoche devised an ingenious method of reducing the country without laying it waste, by depriving it of its arms, and taking parts of its produce for the supply of the Republican army. In the first place, he persisted in the maintenance of entrenched camps, some of which, situated on the Sèvre, separated Charette from Stofflet, while others covered Nantes, the Coast, and Les Sables. He then formed a circular line, which was supported by the Sèvre and the Loire, and tended to envelop progressively the whole country. This line was composed of very strong posts, connected by patrols, so as to leave no free space by which an enemy, who was at all numerous, could pass. These posts were directed to occupy every hamlet and village, and to disarm them. To accomplish this they were to seize the cattle, which usually grazed together, and the corn stowed away in the barns; they were also to secure the principal inhabitants; they were not to restore the cattle and the corn nor release the persons taken as hostages till the peasants should have voluntarily delivered up their arms. Now, as the Vendéans cared much more about their cattle and their corn than about the Bourbons and Charette, they could not fail to surrender their arms. In order not to be over-reached by the peasants, who might give up a few wretched muskets and keep the others, the officers charged with the disarming were to demand the list of enrolment kept in every parish, and to require as many muskets as there were persons enrolled. In default of these registers, it was recommended to them to make an estimate of the population, and to require a number of muskets equal to one-fourth of the male inhabitants. After receiving the arms, they were faithfully to restore the cattle and the corn, with the exception of a part to be levied by the name of a tax, and to be collected in magazines formed on the rear of that line. Hoche had directed that the inhabitants should be treated with the utmost mildness, and that the most scrupulous punctuality should be observed in restoring their cattle, their corn, and especially their hostages.

He had particularly recommended to the officers to have intercourse with them, to treat them well, to send them even sometimes to his headquarters, and to make them presents of corn and other things. He had also enjoined the greatest respect to be paid to the Curés. "The Vendéans," said he, "have but one real sentiment, that is, attachment to their priests. These latter want nothing but protection and tranquillity; let us ensure both to them, let us add some benefits, and the affections of the country will be restored to us."

That line, which he called the line of disarming,

was to envelop Lower Vendée circularly, to advance by degrees, and at length to embrace the whole of it. As it advanced, it left behind it the disarmed country, reduced, nay even reconciled with the Republic. It moreover protected it against a return of the insurgent chiefs, who usually punished submission to the Republic and the surrender of arms by devastations. Two moveable columns preceded it, to fight those chiefs and to seize them, if possible; and, cooping them up more and more, it could not fail at last to enclose and secure them. The utmost vigilance was recommended to all the commandants of posts to keep them constantly connected by means of patrols, and to prevent the armed bands from breaking through the line and again carrying on the war behind them. But, in spite of all their caution, it was nevertheless possible that Charette and some of his partisans might elude the vigilance of the posts and pass the line of disarming; yet even in this case they could not pass with more than a few persons, and they would find themselves in disarmed districts, restored to tranquillity and security, pacified by kind treatment, and intimidated besides by the vast net of troops which encompassed the country. The case of a revolt on the rear was provided against. Hoche had given orders that one of the moveable columns should immediately fall back upon the insurgent commune, and that, to punish it for not having surrendered all its arms, and having again made use of them, its cattle and corn should be taken away and its principal inhabitants seized. The effect of these punishments was certain, and dispensed with justice; they were calculated to inspire, not hatred, but a salutary fear.

Hoche's plan was immediately carried into execution in the months of Brumaire and Trimaire (November and December).

The line of disarming, passing through St. Giles, Légé, Montaigne, and Chantonnay, formed a semicircle, the right extremity of which was supported by the sea and the left by the river Lay, and which was progressively to hem Charette in impracticable morasses. It was chiefly by the manner of its execution that a plan of this nature could succeed. Hoche directed his officers by luminous instructions, full of sound reason, and was indefatigable in attending to all the details. It was not merely a war; it was a great military operation, which required as much prudence as energy. The inhabitants soon began to surrender their arms, and to become reconciled to the Republican troops. Hoche granted relief to the indigent from the magazines of the army; he himself saw the inhabitants detained as hostages, caused them to be kept a few days, and sent them away satisfied. To some he gave cockades, to others police caps; sometimes even corn to such as had none for sowing their fields. He was in correspondence with the curés, who placed great confidence in him, and acquainted him with all the secrets of the country.

He thus began to acquire a great moral influence, a real power, which it was requisite to terminate such a war. Meanwhile the magazines, formed in the rear of the line of disarmament, gradually filled; great numbers of cattle were collected, and the army began to live in abundance through the simple expedient of levying a tax and fines in kind.

Charette had sought refuge in the woods with 150 men as desperate as himself. Sapinaud, who at his instigation had again taken arms, offered to lay them down a second time on the mere condition that his life should be spared. Stofflet, pent up in Anjou with his minister, Bernier, collected there all the officers who had forsaken Charette and Sapinaud, and strove to enrich himself with their spoils. At his headquarters at Lavior he kept a sort of court, composed of emigrants and officers. He enrolled men and levied contributions, upon pretext of organizing the territorial guards. Hoche watched him very attentively, hemmed him in more by entrenched camps, and threatened him with a speedy disarming on the first sign of dissatisfaction. An expedition ordered by Hoche into Le Laroux, a district which had a sort of independent existence, without obliging either the Republic or any chief, struck terror into Stofflet. Hoche sent this expedition to bring away the wine and the corn in which Le Laroux abounded, and of which the city of Nantes was utterly destitute. Stofflet was alarmed and solicited an interview with Hoche for the purpose of protesting his adherence to the treaty, interceding for Sapinaud and the Chouans, making himself in some sort the mediator of a new pacification, and securing by these means the continuance of his influence. He wished also to discover Hoche's intentions in regard to him. Hoche enumerated the grievances of the Republic and intimated that, if he afforded an asylum to all the brigands, if he continued to levy men and money, if he was determined to be anything more than the temporary chief of the police at Anjou, and to play the part of Prince, he would carry him off immediately and then disarm his province. Stofflet promised the utmost submission, and retired full of apprehensions respecting the future.

These operations of Hoche in the west commenced the real pacification of La Vendée, which had been so often and so vainly proclaimed.—(Thiers.)

A war of devastation had been previously tried and had failed. The Republicans had formed fourteen entrenched camps, which enclosed the whole insurgent country, and from them had issued incendiary columns to burn the woods, hedges, copses, and even the villages themselves. All had been in vain. The Vendéans had not ceased to cultivate their lands amidst these horrid scenes. On a signal from their chiefs they would suddenly assemble, and falling upon the rear of the camps storm them, or, allowing the columns to advance, they rushed upon them when they had got into the heart of the country, and, if they succeeded in breaking them, they put to death all, to the very last man.

Acting on the experiences thus graphically described by M. Thiers the pacification of the Burmese Empire was systematically undertaken. It was, in the first place, quartered off into large districts, six in number, the pacification of each district being allotted to one brigade, the total force employed being 25,599 men.

The size of these districts varied according to circumstances, the largest area entrusted to one brigade being 16,820 square miles, and the smallest area 3,675 square miles. The total extent of country to be pacified was somewhat greater than the whole of France. Each brigade worked independently, except where joint action on contiguous boundaries was required.

From the report of Sir William Lockhart, who commanded one of the brigades, we find that up to the time when an organized system of pacification was decided upon, the paucity of men and the insufficiency of transport had seriously crippled the various commanders. Troops were unable to pursue and hunt down the rebels, as rations could not be carried for more than two or three days' supply. The enemy, therefore, invariably after a skirmish, more or less stubborn, evacuated his position only to reoccupy it on the retirement of the troops. The density of the jungle and the want of mounted men to operate in the more open districts saved the enemy from any very heavy loss during their retreats. The people of the country only recognized the patent fact that the rebels were strong enough to levy and collect the taxes and impress men and labour whenever they wished to do so, whilst the mere handful of British troops had invariably to retire after a hollow victory, often harassed by the rebels on their return march. Under these circumstances it was but natural that the people of the country were unable to realize that the occupation of the country by the British would be permanent. They therefore stood aloof watching events before throwing in their lot with either side, unless forced to do so. The rebels' method of rationing themselves was to sit down in some rich village, or group of villages, and to remain there, unless disturbed, till provisions began to run short. They then either removed their camp to some similar spot, or sent out strong foraging parties of about a hundred men to distant villages, and attacking in the day time when the men were in the fields, seized all they wanted.

It was the business of the different columns into which each brigade was split up to search out these snug retreats and to attack, kill, capture, or disperse the bands of rebels encamped in them. This in itself required the greatest skill, for the pursuit of bands of rebels, and the capture of their leaders, in roadless districts abounding in hiding places, surrounded by belts of dense jungle, often many miles in depth, the approaches through which were known to few but the rebels themselves, was no easy task. Add to this the difficulty of obtaining information from a population long held in terror under the relentless rule of the very rebel leaders now to be hunted down, and whose punishment for information against them was crucifixion, and it will be seen that each minor operation was one beset with countless difficulties. So complicated indeed was the problem on many occasions that it was found impossible to give any detailed instructions whatever, and therefore young officers gained the fine experience of being obliged to act entirely on their own responsibility. As the operation advanced, its success necessarily depended much on good fortune, but more on the individual energy and resource of the officers selected to lead. In all, upwards of one hundred separate and distinct engagements with the enemy took place during the systematic pacification of the country. These engagements resulted, as a rule, from night marches and the surprise of villages, from attacks on stockades, from ambuscades laid by the enemy and counter ambuscades made by our troops, and from attacks of the enemy on convoys, and on rear and advance guards actions. Through this maze of small fights the great end was surely and steadily kept in view. The circle of pacification gradually extended in each district, the disarmament of the populace went steadily on, and as the meshes closed slowly but resistlessly round the few desperate bands that remained, peace, tranquillity, and prosperity grew behind the solid wall of just and humane government which in each district the vigorous action of the troops gradually built up. The undertaking was a long and trying one, occupying several years, but the inevitable reward was eventually reached in the complete pacification of the country and the inauguration of a new era of peace and prosperity to a hitherto down-trodden race. To give a detailed account of all or even of a moiety of the numerous engagements which each in their degree contributed to the ultimate result, would be out of the question; but amongst the instances of minor operations given in other chapters will be found numerous instances of engagements fought in the Burmese forests, in the attack on Burmese stockades, and the surprise of Burmese villages.

CHAPTER IV.

Defensive Warfare.

In Asiatic warfare, as carried on between a European Power and the natives of an Eastern country, the initiative is in the large majority of instances taken by the former. But if future events should bring two European Powers into collision in Asia, one or other must of necessity play a defensive part. In such a campaign the great physical features that exist, in all possible theatres of operations, would naturally play a conspicuous part. Vast ranges of mountains, immense rivers, and great forests might each and all come into the theatre of operations, whilst the forces employed on either side could not, from various causes, be so great as those employed by belligerent Powers on battle fields nearer home. The problem before each would therefore possess elements essentially different from those which obtain in Europe, the main feature of such a problem being the prosecution of a campaign, either offensive or defensive, by a comparatively small body of troops in an immense theatre of war. To a strategist or tactician accustomed to European methods, European numbers, and European tactical features, a campaign in Asia has many strange and startling novelties. Positions which an Army Corps would defend or attack in Europe may have to be entrusted to the prowess of a single battalion. The mere passage of obstacles may cause a dispersion of force which would be dangerous were not the opponent committed to a corresponding disintegration. We have only to look at a great river like the Indus or a great mountain range like the Himalayas, where the points of passage are hundreds of miles apart, to thoroughly appreciate this difficulty. It is not, however, here intended to enter into great strategical operations either offensive or defensive, but rather to deal with tactical details which come within the ken of every soldier. The defensive rôle is, as we have shown, not a usual one for a British force fighting in Asia; the dash and energy of the national character will on the contrary very generally throw the onus of defence on the enemy. It stands to reason therefore that our opponents have during the course of decades gained a considerable amount of experience in the difficult art of fighting defensive battles, and in defending mountain ranges and great forests. Fighting as these tribes do against superior weapons, superior discipline, and vastly superior organization, the stand they make is worthy of every admiration, and the methods employed by them often afford lessons useful even to the most highly trained troops.

Before proceeding to deal with actual instances of defensive operations, great or small, it may not therefore be inappropriate to examine, as an object lesson, the tactical methods of these semi-barbarous tribesmen.

In the defence of a mountain barrier it will generally be found that unless religious motives or tribal pride intervene, the outer barrier is not seriously defended. The reason for this is that, knowing the superiority in armament which he has to meet, he eschews a decisive opening battle. On the other hand, he knows that every mile the civilized force advances into his country the more open it is with its trains and convoys to the peculiar form of reprisals in which the guerilla tribesman is no mean proficient. When in the spring of 1895 it was necessary to despatch a force from Peshawur to the relief of Chitral, the first march beyond the British border brought the division to a mountain barrier. Behind this barrier lay the Swat Valley. We had no cause of war with the Swatis, nor they with us, yet when, as a matter of extreme urgency, the British Government asked for a temporary right of way through their country, and offered to pay heavily for the favour, tribal pride, egged on by the sneers of neighbouring clans, refused to grant the concession. We had therefore to assume the rôle of belligerents, and in this case the Swatis stoutly defended the outer barrier of their country. The more usual method would have been to have made merely a show of defence, to have left some passes unguarded and the rest weakly so, and when the British forces were thoroughly committed, and perhaps somewhat dispersed in their arduous struggle over the mountains, to gather in numbers from every rock and village and descend sword in hand with a mighty rush on the most vulnerable points.

Though it is opposed to the strict notions of civilized warfare to abandon without a struggle so formidable an outer barrier as a mountain range, yet a lesson may be learnt from the barbarian who grasps the fact that an invader is at no times more vulnerable than when he is astride of a formidable obstacle like a mountain range.

The border tribesman of India fully accepts the principle that the art of fighting a defensive campaign in a mountainous region does not necessarily consist exclusively or even mainly in fighting defensive battles. He fights no battles if they can possibly be avoided, but remains an ever present, ever formidable, and ever active belligerent, ready to seize and ready to profit by such military blunders as his opponent may happen to make. Here again it is possible to deduce a right line of conduct from our own experiences, to dovetail together the civilized and uncivilized methods of war, and to evolve therefrom defensive tactics peculiarly suitable to the mixed nationalities which compose the Indian Army. Whilst the steady-going British and Sikh and Gurkha soldiers are reserved for the more solid work of a set battle, the Pathans and other hill men, born huntsmen and mountaineers, might well be used to emulate the feats of the most famous guerilla troops, thus adding very materially to the defensive strength of a mountain region.

Defensive warfare in great forests has also peculiar advantages. These advantages it has generally been the privilege of our troops to see from the most unfavourable point of view—the point of view of those undertaking offensive operations. We say privileged, for no lesson is so easily learnt as that taught by viewing an operation from the least favourable point of view. Undoubtedly in operations which aim at defending a forest-covered frontier, the necessary disintegration of the defensive units detracts much from the possibility of combined or concentrated action. Yet it must be remembered that this disadvantage is perhaps in an enhanced degree shared by the opponent. In really thick forest, lines of approach are well known and well defined, and are as often as not single-file tracks with no lateral communications. A single-file track through impenetrable forest is as effectively guarded by a company of Infantry, provided it cannot be turned, as by an Army Corps, and the largest force taking the offensive is of no more avail than a handful of men if fighting is only possible on so narrow a front as is afforded by a single-file track.

It will however rarely be found that a forest is so thick that barricades and entrenchments barring direct roads cannot, with time, be turned. In the systematic defence of a great forest this danger would have to be kept constantly in view, for though the felling of trees would warn the defenders of an extensive flanking manœuvre, yet it would in many cases be quite possible for small parties of the enemy, either by day or night, to creep silently round the flanks and take the defensive barricade in rear. In dealing with woods and copses it is an accepted axiom that the best position for defending them is by taking up a position along the threatened edge, placing entrenchments so as to bar all means of ingress. Theoretically the same course of reasoning, with the intent to keep the enemy exposed in the open whilst our own troops are covered, applies to great forests. But when the size of a forest is such that it must cease to be considered a tactical feature and enters into the larger field of stategy, it is not always possible to act on this principle. Taking, for instance, the great forest-covered continent which is formed by Burmah and Siam, to hold the outer edge of such vast tracts would necessitate a dispersion of force not commensurate with the advantage gained. But though it may be impossible, owing to its extent, to hold the outer edge of a forest, this does not preclude the application of the same principle on a smaller scale within the forest itself. Thus the enemy's objective would be one or two important points within the defender's line, and this might be a seaport, or the capital of the country, or a strategical point necessary for the further prosecution of the campaign. The object of the defenders will therefore be gained if a successful defence of these points is achieved.

An indispensable factor in the successful defence of a forest is the construction of good lateral communications where such do not already exist. In this connection it will be noticed that a navigable river, or series of rivers, running parallel to and within the line of defence, will be of the greatest value, not only as a means of lateral communication, but also because each in its turn will afford to a defender the same advantage which accrues to the holder of the outer edge of a forest. With this further advantage, however, that on the enemy falls the onus of not only forcing a river, but at the same time the border of the wood. It must, nevertheless, be borne in mind that the balance of advantage will be forfeited unless all important points of passage are not only guarded, but the forest cleared away on the enemy's bank at those points, so as to expose him to fire when coming out to force the passage. This rule of course applies only to narrow rivers, where the opposite bank is out of effective rifle range.

It will very generally be found where rivers running parallel to the line of defence exist, that parallel ranges of hills will also be found, and these again furnish further features for assisting in the interior defence of a great forest, the outer edge having perforce been abandoned.

To descend to minor matters in connection with the defence of a forest, and the construction of cover for the defenders. In a forest the first things to hand for the construction of barricades, stockades, and defences generally are the trees close at hand. Until quite recently excellent cover was afforded by felled trees, but it must in future be taken into consideration that bullets with the penetration of the Lee-Metford bullet pass through thick logs with ease, and that, therefore, an earthen parapet will in future be required in all cases where wooden defences are used. Comparatively thin logs, if filled in with two feet of earth or one foot of gravel, will suffice for the purpose. As has been mentioned, the lines of approach will generally be along well-defined tracks, which can be obstructed for miles with all those obstacles which civilized ingenuity has been able to produce. To these may be added one or two devices which have been learnt from Burmans and other forest-born nationalities, such as pitfalls carefully concealed, and deep enough and broad enough to form a serious obstacle even after discovery, and bamboo spikes point upwards concealed in tufts of grass along the borders of the track. These spikes will penetrate the sole of a soldier's ammunition boot, and, of course, cause instant and severe lameness to a horse or pack animal. Where the track passes along the bank of a river or steep hillside it is a common device amongst forest-born tribes and mountaineers to cut the path away and to entangle and obstruct the adjacent slope, so that hours and days, or, if the path is on the face of a cliff, even weeks may be required to repair the damage. Such a device comes within the same category as does the destruction of a bridge. If there is no chance of the path being required for offensive movements in the immediate future, well and good; if, however, there is any doubt on the point so drastic a remedy is hardly advisable.

A very deadly and effective defensive measure employed by the tribesmen of some mountain districts is the establishment of stone-shoots. They find a place where a precipitous incline drops, if possible at some unexpected and exposed corner, on to the path beneath. On the hill above a great collection of boulders obtained close at hand is made, and the moment the enemy appears a continuous and deadly storm of missiles comes hailing down the hill. A stone-shoot of this description is quite impassable for troops as long as it is garrisoned, and the garrison is very generally so placed as to be invisible from the path below and is often unturnable from any direction. A stone-shoot may therefore be placed amongst the list of effective obstacles open to a force placed on its defence in a hill district, whether forest-covered or bare.

So much for the general subject of defensive warfare in so far as it affects the frontiers of our possessions in India. It remains to examine such occasions as have occurred in recent years where a British force, either large or small, has been placed in a position where a defensive attitude was imperative.

Though as has been elsewhere stated to attack, whatever the disparity in numbers, has become an article of faith in the Indian Army, yet it must so happen that bodies of troops, either great or small, have for a time to stand on the defensive when either waiting for a favourable season to resume the offensive, or when detachments temporarily isolated have to hold their own till succour arrives. The best known modern instance, as far as Indian wars are concerned, of a large force standing on the defensive, awaiting the development of events, was at Kabul in December, 1879.

The British force consisted of two brigades of Infantry, one brigade of Cavalry, and three batteries of Artillery, in all some 7,000 fighting men and 24 guns.

This force, under the command of Sir Frederick Roberts, had in the autumn crossed the Shuturgurdan Pass, had won the victory of Charasia, captured Kabul, and dealt out punishment to those implicated in the treacherous murder of Sir Louis Cavagnari, the British envoy, and his gallant escort of 75 men of the Guides. From reasons of policy the force was ordered to remain on in the Afghan capital during the winter. Early in December, with little or no warning, a general rising of the nation took place, and Sir Frederick Roberts found himself faced by from 30,000 to 50,000 fanatical warriors, stirred up to the highest pitch of religious excitement, and filled with the desperate determination to repeat the massacre of 1840, and to extirpate the infidel invader.

Sir Frederick Roberts at once concentrated his forces, and true to our traditions in the East boldly attacked the enemy, who occupied in great force the rocky and precipitous hills which surround the valley in which the city of Kabul lies. Though vastly superior in numbers, the enemy was again and again heavily defeated, and the heights scaled and captured. But here climatic as well as prudential considerations came in. It was now midwinter, these heights were some 7,000 feet high, and the cold so intense that it was impossible to keep troops on the top of them at night, even if such a dispersion of a small force in face of superior numbers had been tactically sound. Thus it came to this pass, that though by day the troops might storm and capture the heights, they had to evacuate them again at nightfall, with the result that the enemy would reoccupy them and the battle would have to be fought over again next day. Under these circumstances, and knowing that from lack of supplies these great gatherings must dwindle away after keeping the field for ten days or a fortnight, Sir Frederick Roberts skilfully withdrew his entire force, occupied the walled enclosure called Sherpur, and determined to act on the defensive until the enemy had frittered away his forces in useless assaults. Further delay would give the enemy's commissariat time to exhaust itself, whilst opportunity would be given for British reinforcements from Jellalabad to break through the interrupted communications and come to his assistance.

Sherpur may be described as parallelogram, whose northern side is formed by the Bimaru ridge, a range of low but steep isolated hills rising some 300 feet above the surrounding plain, and running almost due east and west for a distance (including slopes at either end) of 2,500 yards. The southern face is a continuous and massive wall, 16 feet high, pierced at intervals of about 700 yards by three gateways, which again are protected by lofty circular bastions. Between these gates and also at the corners are a series of lower bastions, which give an admirable flanking fire. The length of the southern side slightly exceeds 2,650 yards. The western flank is constructed on a precisely similar plan, saving that its northern extremity had been much damaged by a recent explosion. This flank is about 1,000 yards in length. On the east the defences were much weaker, the original design remaining uncompleted, and the wall, which was intended to resemble those on the other faces, was only built to a height of seven feet. This wall, after bending outwards to include Bimaru village, joins the eastern slope of the Bimaru ridge.*

This enclosure had been built by the Amir Shere Ali for his own troops.

It will be noticed that the size of the place was its great weakness, considering the smallness of the British force defending it. But no other position was available, and it was impossible to cut off part of the enclosure without at the same time surrendering a portion of the Bimaru hill, any part of which occupied by the enemy would have made the remainder of Sherpur completely untenable.

The country in the immediate vicinity of Sherpur may be thus described. To the north the Bimaru ridge slopes into a perfectly level and open plain, one and a half miles wide, on the far side of which lies the Bimaru lake, a quarter to half a mile broad and three miles long, running east and west, parallel with the Bimaru ridge. This side might therefore be described as perfectly safe. On the other three sides lies a fairly open and cultivated country, intersected by small watercourses and small mud-wall enclosures and studded with villages and mud forts, some of which lay inconveniently close to the defences. It had been contemplated to destroy these so as to form a clear glacis round the defences, but the pressure of even more important work, the collection of supplies,

* Sir F. Roberts' report.

and the provision of shelter from the snow for the troops, combined with the scarcity of labour and the suddenness of the uprising, made it impossible to effect such extensive demolitions in the time available.

The defence was divided into five sections, each placed under the command of a general or other senior officer, and a central reserve was placed in a suitable position near the middle of the inner slope of Bimaru.

Telegraphic communication was established between the Headquarter Gate and each section, and intercommunication between sections was kept up by means of visual signalling.

A laager, made of captured Afghan gun carriages and timbers, was constructed at the north-west corner, which, as above mentioned, had been partially destroyed by an explosion, thus closing the gap at this corner. The ground in the immediate front of the laager was strengthened by means of abattis and wire entanglements.

To furnish flank fire along the western and northern faces of Sherpur, a small village called Mustaufi, which lay just outside the defences, was held as an independent post.

On the Bimaru heights six towers, or block-houses, were built, connected one with the other by a line of shelter trenches which ran along the whole length of the ridge. The front of the shelter trenches was protected by abattis, and gun-pits were made at important points. In order to strengthen the north-east corner, a 2-gun battery was thrown up on the eastern slopes of Bimaru ridge and connected with the tower above and the village below. Bimaru village was loop-holed, the outlying buildings to its front made defensible, and the open space to the north-east obstructed with abattis and wire entanglements. The low wall of the eastern face of the cantonments was raised by logs of wood, the ground to the front here, as elsewhere, being faced with abattis.

The siege commenced on December 14th, on which day the enemy seized and occupied the Bala Hissar and city of Kabul, which had been abandoned by the British troops. On December 15th the telegraph line was broken, and Sir Frederick Roberts was practically cut off from his base in India. During the 15th and 16th all hands were occupied in strengthening the defences of Sherpur, and the gunners and artificers were busy preparing the captured heavy guns and ammunition for service. The enemy on these days were so busy looting the city that they made no serious attacks. They obtained, amongst other things, 130 tons of powder and 100,000 rounds of Snider ammunition, which materially strengthened their hands.

The 17th December was marked by a hostile demonstration against the east and west faces, large bodies of the enemy assembling on the neighbouring heights, some 2,000 to 2,500 yards distant, at which ranges the artillery of the defence engaged them, but no important attack was made. On the 18th, however, shortly before noon, the enemy in great strength moved out of Kabul city, first occupied the hills to the south and west of Sherpur, and then, utilizing the ample cover afforded by the walls, ditches, and villages in front of the southern wall and south-west bastion, pushed their attack up to within 400 yards of the works in the face of a heavy artillery fire. They were, however, at this point checked by the rifle fire poured on them by picked shots from the British troops, and contented themselves with a dropping fire till nightfall. After dark, however, they pushed forward and occupied two forts which it had been impossible to destroy, and which lay only a few hundred yards distant from the eastern face of Sherpur.

Early on the 19th, General Baker, with 800 men and two guns, was ordered out to capture and destroy these forts, which he succeeded in doing, blowing in their front faces and driving out the enemy. Throughout the day the enemy kept up a constant fire from all sides, and several casualties occurred amongst the besieged. During the 20th the enemy employed the same tactics, keeping themselves well under cover. The British loss so far amounted to 77 killed, including 8 officers, and 220 wounded, including 15 officers. On the 21st the Afghans showed signs of special activity, and on that day large numbers of them moved out of the city, and, passing round to the eastward of Sherpur, occupied the numerous forts in that direction in very great force. It became apparent that this movement was preparatory to an attack from that quarter, and at the same time information was received from spies that the enemy was preparing escalading ladders with a view to storming the southern and western walls. But no attack in force was made on this date, and merely desultory and isolated attacks continued throughout this day and the 22nd.

On the night of the 22nd, however, precise information was received that a grand attack would be delivered at dawn on the 23rd, the signal for attack being given by lighting a bonfire on the Asmai heights.

It was further reported that the main attack would be made against the eastern face, which was certainly the weakest, supported by a false attack on the southern wall. The day chosen was the last day of the Mahomedan Mohurrum, and the flames of fanaticism were still further fanned by the knowledge that the aged priest, Mushk-i-Alam, would with his own hand light the signal beacon at dawn on the Asmai heights. The British troops were under arms at a very early hour on the 23rd, and the signal beacon on the heights shortly before daybreak announced that the decisive moment had arrived.

A heavy fire was immediately opened by the enemy against the southern and eastern faces, and by 7 a.m. an attack in force against the eastern side was fully developed, whilst a very large number of the enemy, provided with scaling ladders, were drawn up under the cover of garden walls to the south. From 7 a.m. to 10 a.m. the fight went briskly on, repeated attempts being made by the enemy to carry the low eastern wall by escalade. But though they with great bravery repeatedly reached the abattis, they were again and again mown down by the deadly fire of the besieged, and forced to desist. The brunt of the attack fell on the Guides and the 67th Foot. Soon after 10 a.m. a lull took place, but at 11 a.m. the fight again grew hot, although not marked with the determination of the first attack. Seeing that the Afghans were much shaken, Sir Frederick Roberts determined to boldly take the offensive and to turn the hitherto passive defence into an active one. Accordingly three regiments of Cavalry and a battery of Artillery issued forth from the entrenchments, and falling upon the enemy scattered them in every direction, their dispersion being accelerated by the news that British reinforcements from India were within striking distance.

On the morning of December the 24th, not a single Afghan was to be found in the adjacent villages or visible on the surrounding hills. A British force of 7,000 men had therefore, placed in by no means a model position for defence, withstood for eleven days the assaults of ten times their number, and in the end defeated with great loss and scattered to the four winds the hosts of their enemies.

From this and other instances it will be noted that in taking up a defensive position it rarely occurs that a model position offers itself for occupation. Indeed, we may go a step further and note that it is not uncommon to find that a defensive force is often compelled to take up a position in which the disadvantages appear to overwhelm the advantages. In Sherpur we find that 7,000 men had to hold defences the perimeter of which was over 7,000 yards, whereas a garrison of threefold strength would not have been too much. Forts, villages, mud walls, and irrigation ditches gave ample shelter on three sides to the besiegers up to within a few hundred yards of the works, and we may note that theoretically the position is endangered when the besiegers gain a firm footing within 400 yards of it. The interior of the defences was so open and devoid of cover that not only were constant casualties occurring amongst troops moving about, but the defenders of one side could be taken in reverse by long range fire that cleared the parapet behind them.

The instruction usually given to British officers takes the form of asking them to select a position and to put it into a state of defence. It would perhaps be more practical to give them such apparently hopeless positions as may be forced upon them and ask them to do the best with them. An officer of ordinary common sense can choose a more or less model position, but warfare, and perhaps more especially Asiatic warfare, if we may judge from the experience of the past, rarely affords such an opportunity.

But defensive operations on so large a scale as this are exceptional. It is more usual to find the defensive force a small one, consisting of a mere handful of men left temporarily isolated. The measures for defence employed on these occasions are very instructive, and the experience gained will be of use to young officers placed in like positions, as they may be any day on any portion of the Indian frontier.

Let us take the defence of Chitral Fort by a small force consisting of six British officers, a company of the 14th Sikhs numbering 99, and 301 men of the Maharaja of Kashmir's Infantry, during the spring of 1895. The Fort was of native build, eighty yards square, with walls twenty-five feet high and about eight feet thick. At each corner was a tower some twenty feet higher than the wall, and outside the north face, on the river bank, stood a fifth tower constructed to guard the waterway. On the east face a garden wall runs out for a distance of 140 yards, and forty yards from the S.E. tower was a summer-house. On the north and west faces were stables and other outhouses. The fort was built of rude masonry, kept together, not by cement or mortar of any description, but by a cradle work of beams placed longitudinally and transversely. It was situated on the right bank of the Chitral River, some fifty yards from the water's edge. It was commanded on nearly all sides at close ranges from the slopes of the surrounding mountains.

It is not necessary to enter here into the history of events which brought this small force into Chitral; suffice it to say that the country had hitherto been perfectly friendly, and that the storm burst so suddenly that the force had to take to the only available shelter which was furnished by this rough fort, and was immediately so closely hemmed in as to be unable even to destroy the garden walls and outhouses which gave shelter to the enemy close up to the fort walls. To add to the difficulty of the position high trees at close range completely commanded the interior of the fort.

Captain Townsend, who was in command, took such

steps as were possible to make the place tenable. A covered way was made from the water tower down to the river's edge. Planks, beams of wood, doors, mule saddles, boxes and sacks filled with earth were arranged as parados as a protection from the reverse fire which poured in from every side. But there was a great lack of solid materials for constructing these parados, and the deficiency was as far as possible made good by hanging up carpets, tents, and curtains so that protection from view at any rate might be obtained.

The besiegers were well versed in the art of attacking such forts as Chitral, for many of them had spent their lives in attacking and defending similar ones, consequently they at once grasped the fact that to cut off the water supply was the first thing to be done. On the third night of the siege therefore they made a determined attack on the water tower, captured it and set it on fire. But the garrison, pouring in steady volleys at close range, drove off the attacking party and extinguished the flames. To guard against similar night attacks, platforms were built out from the parapet, and on these fires were kept burning to light up the ground around the fort. On the ninth night another formidable attack was made, but was repulsed with slaughter.

A few days later came the disheartening news that reinforcements from Mastuj with a heavy convoy of ammunition and engineer's stores had been defeated, and that the ammunition and stores had fallen into the hands of the enemy. However, nothing daunted, the garrison set to work to strengthen in every possible way their defences. The men were now on half rations of grain stuff and without meat of any sort. The officers killed their ponies and salted them down. For the next few days and nights the rain poured in torrents, doing much damage to the walls, a large piece of the parapet on the west front subsiding, and giving the garrison much work in rebuilding it. On the 29th March, the twenty-sixth day of the siege, a Union Jack made up from the red cloth of the sepoys' turbans and other material was hoisted on the top of the highest tower, and from that time onward the luck of the garrison began to turn.

Repeated attempts had been made to communicate with the outside world, but without success, nor could news of the relief columns reach the garrison, though every device was tried, even to shooting arrows into the fort with letters attached to them, but to no purpose.

On the 31st of March the enemy made a new sangar on the opposite bank of the river, commanding at a range of only 175 yards the spot from whence the garrison drew its water. The only protection which the garrison could put up was a screen of tents, which hid from view the men going down to the water. The enemy were not only advancing their trenches towards the waterway from the opposite bank of the river, but they also commenced the construction of a covered way to the water from their lower sangar, which was only eighty yards off.

On the 5th and 6th April the enemy showed great

activity in the south-east corner of the fort, occupying the summer-house only forty yards distant and constructing a large fascine sangar in front of the main gate at a distance of forty yards only. At these extraordinary close ranges they kept up a galling fire on the loopholes in the fort, and made the lookout work most difficult and dangerous.

At 5 a.m. on the 7th April, a large number of the enemy opened a heavy fire from the trees in front of the north tower, and an attack was made on the covered way to the water. But the steady volleys of the Sikhs drove off the assailants from these points. Meanwhile, however, under cover of the firing, the enemy managed with great boldness to place huge faggots and blocks of wood in a pile against the corner of the gun tower on the south-east, and setting a light to them the tower was soon in a blaze. This was a most serious matter, and Captain Townsend immediately sent up the whole of the inlying picket with their great-coats full of earth, whilst as much water as could be obtained was poured on the flames. A strong wind was blowing at the time, and the tower was under the enemy's searching fire at forty yards range, so that Surgeon-Major Robertson and nine men were shot before the fire was got under. On the evening of the 8th April another attempt was made to set the fort on fire, but was again frustrated. Again, on the night of the 10th, a determined attack was made on the waterway and again repulsed.

On the following day it was noticed that the enemy began playing tomtoms and Pathan pipes in the summer-house and shouting abuse at intervals, but it was not till four days later that a sharp-eared sentry heard the sound of picking in a mine, which operation the noise in the summer-house was intended to cover. On the 17th April it was calculated that the mine had reached within twelve feet of the wall, and it became imperative to make a sortie to destroy it. This desperate enterprise was entrusted to Lieutenant H. K. Harley with a party of 40 Sikhs and 60 Kashmir Infantry. At four o'clock in the afternoon the gate at the east face of the fort was quietly opened, and Lieutenant Harley rushed out at the head of his party, a man on each side of him being immediately knocked over. Dashing into the summer-house he surprised and drove out the garrison, bayoneting thirty-five at the mouth of the mine. But the enemy were now thoroughly aroused, and seeing that the fort must now be weakly guarded, with great judgment made a counter-attack on the waterway. It took Lieutenant Harley the best part of an hour to clear the mine. He then placed 110 pounds of powder which he had brought with him in position and blew up the mine, then collecting his men, dashed back into the fort. His losses were heavy, 21 men being killed or wounded.

This was the forty-sixth day of the siege, and undoubtedly this bold sortie not only saved the garrison from disaster, but had a most disheartening effect on the enemy, for they hereby perceived that the indomitable courage of the garrison was not for a moment dimmed, even after the severe ordeal they had been through. Simultaneously with this severe check came news that the relief columns both from north and south were rapidly approaching; the enemy therefore reluctantly raised the siege and retreated into the mountains.

This is a fine example of a defence carried out under the most disadvantageous conditions that it would be possible to find. The fort was completely commanded on every side, and was for forty-six days under a severe fire from breechloaders as well as muzzle loaders, at ranges so small as to make it a matter of wonder that there were any survivors at all. There has been no practical experience of the effect of rifle fire at ranges varying from 40 to 175 yards. So weak were the walls that they crumbled away before heavy rain, and so awkwardly constructed that until machicouli galleries had been made the defenders could not get a view of the foot of them, with the result that they were on several occasions very nearly burnt out, as was the garrison of the Kabul Embassy on another occasion. The military officer in India has often had to pore over the dry details of text books on fortification, and has probably a hundred times passed wearily over the list of the various domestic articles used in the defence of farm-houses in England, without feeling much stirred with interest, serving as he does in a country where farm-houses do not exist. But here we have illustrated in the most practical way the utilization of resources which, scanty as they are, would be to hand in many defensive posts; stone walls, beams, tents as a screen from view, old ammunition boxes, sacks and great coats, used for carrying earth, and water skins; besides the more scientific use of machicouli galleries and covered ways.

If there was one weak spot in the defensive scheme, it was in the non-utilization of a few old mountain guns which were found in the fort. Undoubtedly it would have been impossible to fire these from the parapet without shaking down the whole wall of the fort, but it would appear to have been not altogether impossible, in the earlier days of the siege, at any rate, to have run out a small work from one of the gates and to have placed a gun or two in it. Military critics who have examined the ground are of opinion that guns thus placed would have made such a close investment of the place impossible. On the other hand, the garrison was barely strong enough to man the walls, there were no trained gunners amongst them, and no doubt the Sikhs felt more confidence in their own weapons than in the working of a gun of which they knew nothing.

THE DEFENCE OF KABUL RESIDENCY.

Let us now turn to the description of the defence of another isolated post against immense odds in a bad position, and where no time was given for improving such defences as there were.

In the summer of 1879 Sir Louis Cavagnari was sent to Kabul as British Resident, with an escort of 50

Infantry and 25 Cavalry of the Guides, under the command of Lieutenant Walter Hamilton, V.C. The Embassy was lodged in an ordinary house in the Bala Hissar Fort, whilst the escort was billeted in huts close at hand. On one side the house was safe, standing as it did on the outer wall of the fort with a sheer drop of from thirty to forty feet. On all other sides the house was perfectly defenceless. It appears that early on the morning of Sept. 3rd, some of the Amirs' Herati regiments came to the Bala Hissar to demand their pay, now long in arrears, from the Amir's Commander-in-Chief. But the exchequer was empty and the troops were turned away. On their way back from the palace they were passing the British Embassy, when from wantonness or bravado they opened fire on the sentry and on some of the men about. The door of the enclosure where the horses were was immediately shut, and the mutineers were remonstrated with, but with no effect. Every moment more troops arrived, and a heavy fire was opened on the devoted building. To this the Guides, nothing loth for a fight, briskly responded, and it seemed at one time that their fine discipline and steady shooting would damp the ardour of the assailants. If it had been necessary to deal only with the original force, without doubt the enemy would have been repulsed; but the sound of firing had brought dense crowds along the narrow streets from every direction, so that, however anxious those in front might have been to retreat, it was impossible for them to do so. Hitherto, however, no impression had been made on the Embassy, and it was decided by the besiegers to bring up some guns which happened to be parked close by. Placing these behind a small wall, a most destructive and deadly fire was opened on the Embassy at a range of only a few yards. Twice Lieut. Hamilton charged out and captured the nearest gun, and twice was beaten back with the loss of all his party. In his third gallant attempt the gun was again captured and dragged some way towards the Embassy door, but before the deed was accomplished Lieut. Hamilton and his men were all killed. Meanwhile the rest of the British officers, of whom there were three—Sir Louis Cavagnari, Mr. Jenkins his assistant, and Dr. Kelly—were all killed or mortally wounded, and the defence devolved on a Sikh native officer, Jemadar Jiwand Sing, of the Guides. Several times during the course of the day, for it was now getting on towards evening, offers had been made to the garrison that their lives would be spared if they would hand over the British officers. The reply to such offers had been a deadly shower of bullets. Even now, when the British officers were no more, the sturdy old Sikh held out.

The garrison was now reduced to a mere handful of men, who were still resolutely holding out, when some of the enemy, creeping along the neighbouring roofs, set fire to the Embassy buildings. After twelve hours of desperate fighting, towards eight o'clock in the evening the buildings became untenable, and the little band of devoted heroes sallied forth and died to a man, fighting to the last against tremendous odds. It was afterwards ascertained that this gallant band of Guides, though itself exterminated, had inflicted a loss on the enemy of 600 men during the day.

THE DEFENCE OF THOBAL.

A fine instance of a successful defence by a small body of troops against vastly superior numbers is afforded by Lieutenant Grant's defence of Thobal.

On March 27th, 1891, news was received at Tamu that a disaster had occurred at Manipur, the capital of a neighbouring semi-independent state, whither Mr. Quinton, the British Commissioner, had proceeded to settle certain political matters. Mr. Quinton was accompanied by four civil officers and had an escort of seven British officers and 454 Gurkhas. The officer commanding at Tamu was Lieutenant C. J. W. Grant, 12th Burmah Infantry; and when the report reached him that the whole party had been massacred, he immediately volunteered to push on to Manipur, in the hope that there might remain some survivors whom he could rescue. His available force consisted of

1 native officer and 30 rifles of the 43rd Gurkhas, with 60 rounds per man (Martini), and

1 native officer and 50 rifles, 12th Burmah Infantry, with 160 rounds per man (Snider).

Of the latter only 20 were old soldiers, the remainder being recruits who had only fired a few rounds of ball ammunition.

From Tamu to Manipur is about fifty-five miles.

Starting at 5.30 a.m. on the 28th, Lieutenant Grant reached the Lokchao River at 5 p.m., having been able only to progress at the rate of a mile an hour. Starting again at 2 a.m. on the 29th, the party got as far as Kongaung, a distance of about ten miles, being occasionally fired at by the enemy. At 11 p.m. the same night the moon rose, and the advance was continued. After proceeding a short distance it was found that the telegraph wire had been cut, taken down from the poles, and twisted about the road. This obstacle caused great delay in the dark. Moreover, trees had been felled across the road, and a hot fire was opened on the party as they cleared away the obstacles. Lieutenant Grant sent small parties to turn the ambushed enemy out of his position, which they did, capturing three guns and a good deal of ammunition.

Pushing on, Lieutenant Grant issued from the hills at 6 a.m., and came in sight of the village of Palel, which was garrisoned by 200 men of the Manipur army. The small British force at once attacked and drove out the Manipuris, capturing a few prisoners and pursuing them for three miles.

Halting that day at Palel, a start was made again at 11 p.m., along the foothills, and across swampy fields. At 5.30 a.m. the party came to some villages, each house standing in a large compound surrounded by a wall, ditch, and hedge.

Attacking these, Lieutenant Grant drove the enemy out of them one after another, till, issuing on the other side, he came to a plain about one thousand yards across. Beyond this was to be seen a bridge on fire, both flanks of it being held by the enemy posted

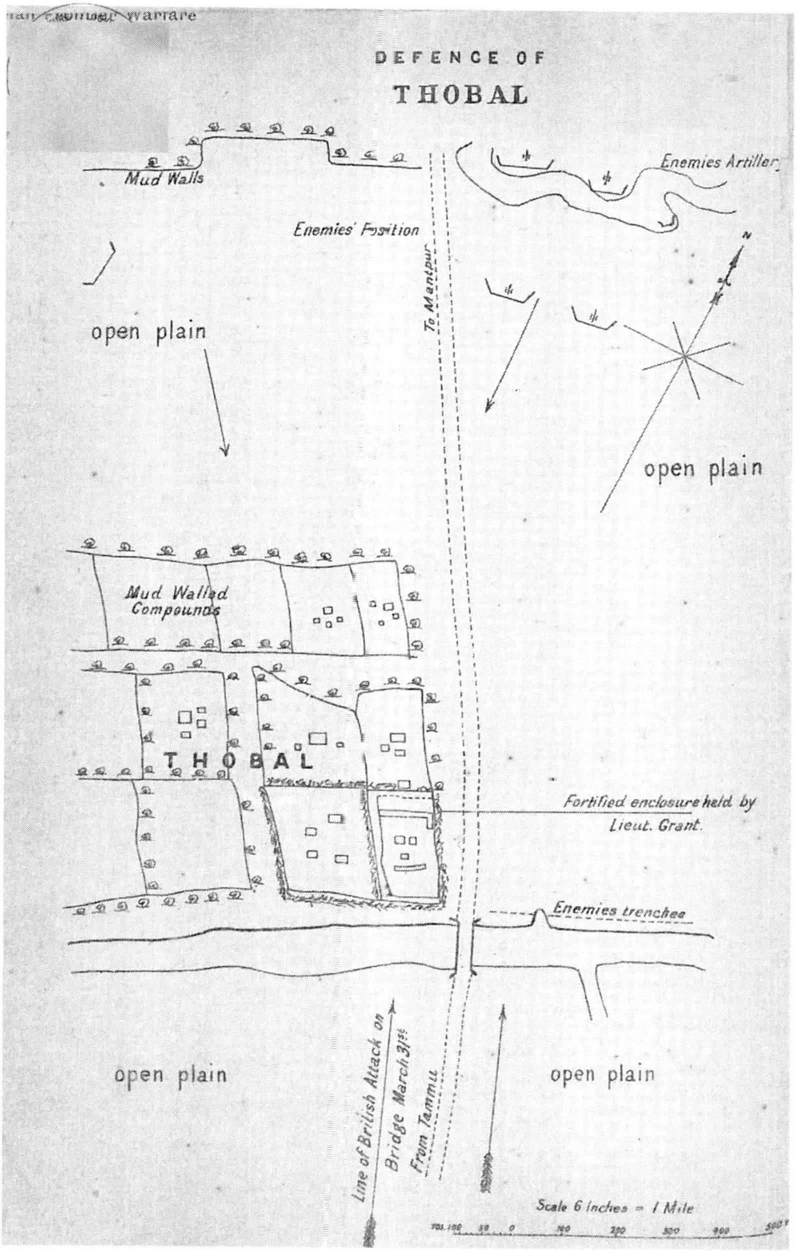
DEFENCE OF
THOBAL
Mud Walls
Enemies' Position
To Manipur
Enemies Artiller
open plain
open plain
Mud Walled
Compounds
THOBAL
Fortified enclosure held by
Lieut. Grant.
Enemies trenchee
open plain
open plain
Line of British Attack on
Bridge March 31st
From Tammu
Scale 6 inches = 1 Mile

in trenches and behind hedges. Lieutenant Grant immediately decided to attack and to attempt to save the bridge. He advanced across the plain with a firing line consisting of two sections of ten men each, each supported by another section of the same strength. The rest of his force, consisting of forty men, he kept in reserve. Advancing boldly under a heavy fire, during which Lieutenant Grant was wounded, they succeeded in working up to within 100 yards of the enemy. Here, the firing line being reinforced, the whole dashed into the river and stormed the enemy's trenches, completely defeating them, and hunting them from enclosure to enclosure. The enemy numbered about 1,000, and are reported to have lost heavily.

Lieutenant Grant was now in possession of the village of Thobal, which lies only about fifteen miles from Manipur; his position was close to the road, and so placed as to form a refuge to any who might have escaped the massacre. The heavy odds against him made it impossible for Lieutenant Grant to advance further, he therefore set to work to entrench himself.

The evening of the 31st was spent in preparing a defensive position, clearing the field of fire and making abattis. Over a ton of rice, and five or six earthenware jars of coarse sugar, were collected as rations for the men. The night passed quietly, but at 6 a.m. on April 1st the enemy were seen advancing in force. Lieutenant Grant, without waiting to be attacked, sent out thirty men to a wall about four hundred yards to his front, and the fire from this point checked the enemy and he retired for a time. At 3 p.m. the enemy advanced again and opened a heavy fire with Martini, Snider, and Enfield rifles, the line attacking being over a mile long. Again occupying the line of wall to his front, Lieutenant Grant held his fire till the enemy reached a point which had been carefully marked as distant 600 yards, whilst preparations for the defence were being made. The severe fire of the garrison at this known range repulsed the attacking force, which fell back, under the protection of its artillery. The enemy's guns now began to bombard the garrison at a range of 1,000 yards. But Lieutenant Grant, judging the distance by sound, poured in volley after volley, and in thirty minutes completely silenced the guns, which were withdrawn to another hill 500 yards further off. Even here, however, the fire of our Martinis found them out, and the guns began firing wildly. Meanwhile the enemy kept up a hot rifle fire, but were again and again driven back when they reached the 600-yard limit. Darkness was now setting in, and the enemy began working round the left flank of the defenders. Lieutenant Grant therefore quietly withdrew his men one by one from their forward position and concentrated them in his entrenched position.

The enemy kept up a heavy fire till 2 a.m., but the garrison, who had to husband every round of ammunition, made no reply. At 3 a.m. the besieged party set to work to further strengthen the defences, using baskets filled with earth, ration bags and sacks filled with sand, as well as abattis. In the course of the day the enemy sent in a flag of truce and made several favourable offers to Lieutenant Grant. These he absolutely refused to accept unless all prisoners still in the hands of the Manipuris were delivered over to him. As a *ruse de guerre*, Lieutenant Grant put on a colonel's badge and passed himself off as the Colonel of his regiment, with a full regiment at his back. So successfully, indeed, did he keep up the *rôle* that even a European prisoner in the enemy's hands was deceived. After three days of fruitless negotiations hostilities were commenced, the enemy at dawn on the 6th April making in great force a determined attack on the position, supporting the advance with the fire of artillery. By 8 a.m. they had pushed the attack home so far as to have seized lines of walls and hedges, which it had been impossible to demolish, as close as 100 yards from the British position. But even thus hemmed closely in on all sides by very superior forces, Lieutenant Grant's resources did not fail him. He boldly decided to make a counter-attack, and with this object in view he crept out with ten Gurkhas, and unobserved, turned the left flank of one of the walls, and falling briskly on the surprised defenders, killed six or seven of them and routed the rest. He then retired to his fortified position. At 11 a.m. it was found necessary to make another counter-attack. Lieutenant Grant again crept out, accompanied by a non-commissioned officer and six Gurkhas. After driving the enemy from one hedge, he discovered a party of about sixty men in a corner behind a wall twenty yards distant. Dashing across this open space under a very hot fire, he, with his party, fell with great fury on the enemy. Lieutenant Grant himself used a 16-bore shot gun loaded with slugs with great effect. After killing eleven of the enemy at this point in a desperate hand-to-hand encounter, and completely routing the rest, of whom a great many were wounded, Lieutenant Grant again retired to his fortified position. On taking stock of his ammunition he found that he had left only fifty rounds per Snider rifle, thirty rounds per Martini-Henri rifle. He was therefore constrained to assume a purely passive defensive, with strict orders that no one was to fire till the enemy was half way across the field of fire. The enemy kept up a continuous but innocuous fire till dark and then retired.

On April 7th large parties of the enemy were seen moving round to the right of the position, which during the day was still further strengthened. No attack was made on the 7th or 8th, and on the 9th April a letter from his official superior reached Lieutenant Grant, forwarded by the enemy, who were apparently glad to get rid of him at any price, ordering him to retire on Tamu, whence a force had been despatched to extricate him. On a dark rainy night, in the midst of a heavy thunderstorm, Lieutenant Grant quietly evacuated his position, and, retiring without loss towards Tamu, was shortly met by the relieving force.

The defence of Thobal is a fine example of what a resolute front and bold leading can do against Asiatics. It must be remembered that the Manipuris had an army, more or less regular, which had originally been trained by Europeans, that they were armed with modern breechloaders, with an unlimited supply of ammunition, and that they had just gained what would by them be considered a signal victory over a strong force of Gurkhas led by British officers. There is much instruction not only in the careful manner in which Lieutenant Grant chose his position and strengthened it, but also as illustrating the great principle that counter-attack is the salt of life to all successful defences. If in any case of defence it would be allowable for a commander to employ a purely passive defence, that case would be when, as in Lieutenant Grant's case, he had only eighty men as against several thousand of the enemy supported by artillery. Yet even here the adherence to this principle, brilliantly bold as it was, brought victory to the little force, and probably helped more than anything to the final repulse of the enemy.

The three instances we have given illustrate defensive operations carried on by small isolated detachments against vastly superior numbers; but it would be leaving the subject incomplete if it were to be closed without some reference to defensive operations on a larger scale.

It may on rare occasions happen that by surprise, or of set purpose, a defensive battle is forced on a British commander. Amongst such battles may be classed the battle of Ahmed Kheyl, a battle which, though long expected, actually took place whilst the British division was on the line of march, and which, from the partially unexpected and extremely rapid flank attack of the enemy, compelled the British flank to fight a defensive battle facing to its flank.

THE BATTLE OF AHMED KHEYL.*

On the 19th of April, 1880, the division under Lieut.-General Sir Donald Stewart, marching from Kandahar towards Kabul, encountered an Afghan force, estimated at 1,000 horse and 12,000 to 15,000 foot, at Ahmed Kheyl, some twenty-three miles south of Ghazni.

For several days previous a hostile force had been seen by the cavalry scouts marching parallel to the route taken by the division and about eight miles distant on the right flank. The country for the last hundred miles passed over by the troops had been almost entirely deserted, so that not only was the supply of the troops arranged for with difficulty, but it was scarcely possible to obtain any intelligence of the character of the opposition that might be offered.

On the 18th of April the camp was at Mushaki. The division marched thence at daylight on the 19th, in the following order:—

(1) The advance guard, consisting of: 689 rifles; 350 lances; 6 guns, R.H.A.

(2) The main body, consisting of the 2nd Infantry Brigade, strength 1,092 rifles, with 349 sabres, and 10 guns, R.A.

(3) The baggage, ammunition, and supply trains, and hospital, guarded by detachments on each flank.

(4) The rear guard, composed of the 1st Infantry Brigade, strength 1,393 rifles, with 316 sabres, and 6 mountain guns, R.A.

* Taken almost verbatim from the Official Account.

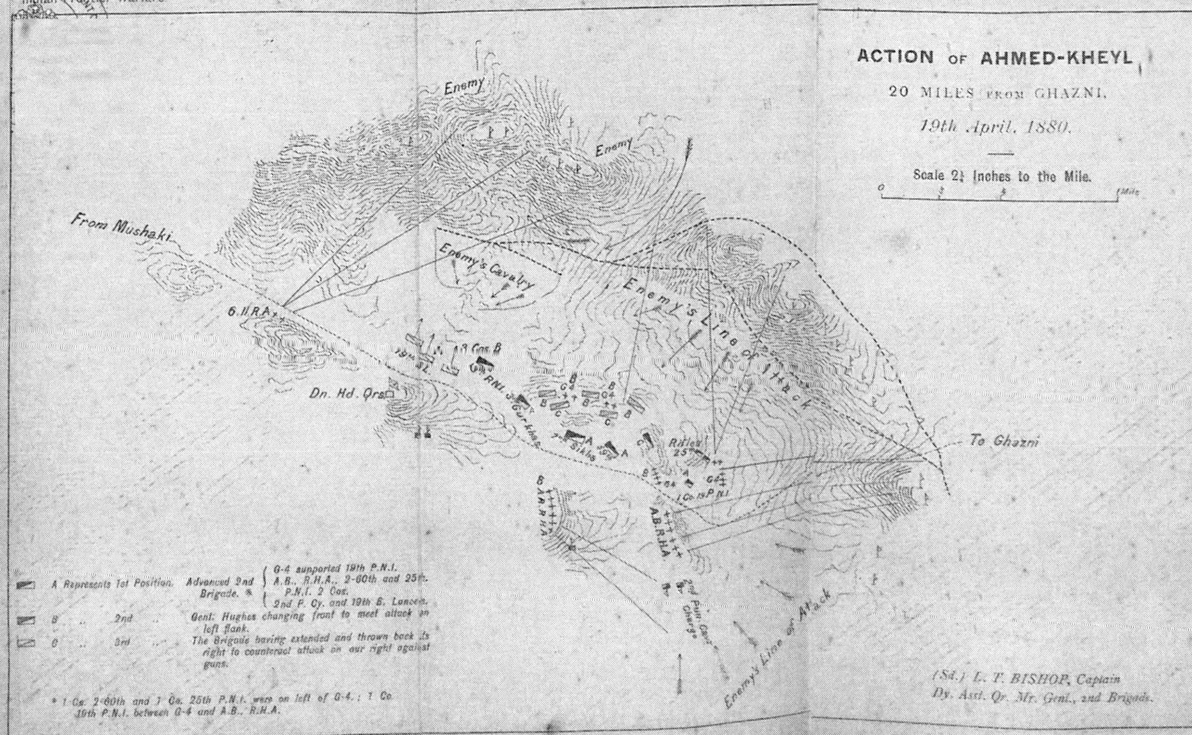
ACTION OF AHMED-KHEYL
20 MILES FROM GHAZNI.
19th April, 1880.
Scale 2¼ Inches to the Mile.
0
Mile
Enemy
Enemy
From Mushaki
Enemy's Cavalry
Enemy's Line of Attack
6.11 R.A.
Dn. Hd. Qrs.
19th B.L.
3 Cos. B
3rd Gurkhas
7th Sikhs
Rifles 25th
G-4
1 Co. 19 P.N.I.
A.B.R.H.A.
B A.B.R.H.A.
To Ghazni
2nd Punj. Cavy. Charge
Enemy's Line of Attack
A Represents 1st Position. Advanced 2nd Brigade. * G-4 supported 19th P.N.I. A.B., R.H.A., 2-60th and 25th P.N.I. 2 Cos. 2nd P. Cy. and 19th B. Lancers.
B .. 2nd .. Genl. Hughes changing front to meet attack on left flank.
C .. 3rd .. The Brigade having extended and thrown back its right to counteract attack on our right against guns.
* 1 Co. 2-60th and 1 Co. 25th P.N.I. were on left of G-4; 1 Co. 19th P.N.I. between G-4 and A.B., R.H.A.
(Sd.) L. T. BISHOP, Captain
Dy. Asst. Qr. Mr. Genl., 2nd Brigade.

To face P. 101

The length of the entire column when on the march was about six miles.

Divisional headquarters, which were with the infan try of the advance guard, had marched about seven miles when the advance guard cavalry reported bodies of the enemy in position three miles ahead. Sir Donald Stewart directed the battalions of the 2nd Brigade, which formed the main body, to form on the left of the road, in line with the Royal Horse Artillery battery, which was in column of route on the road. The cavalry passed to the right, the country on that side being flat and open as far as the Ghazni River, some three miles distant. The 19th Punjab Infantry, which had up to now formed the advance guard, together with the two companies of Sappers, followed in reserve. The two remaining batteries* closed up with the horse battery on the road in column of route. Orders were sent back to the rear guard brigade to send forward a battalion and a half of infantry and two squadrons of Cavalry.

At 8 a.m. the advance was resumed, half a squadron of the 19th Bengal Lancers being sent to cover the left flank of the Infantry brigade, which was now in close proximity to a range of low hills. These hills ran parallel to the line of march for some distance, and then, making a bend round from west to east, crossed the line of advance at right angles. The enemy were seen in position covering the road at the point of passage through the hills, with their right

* G.4, armed with six 9-pounder guns, and 6-11, armed with two 40-pounder guns and two 6·3 in. howitzers.

wing following the run of the hills and flanking the road by which the division would advance.

When within a mile and a half of the enemy, the horse artillery battery and the field battery moved out and took up positions to shell the ridge in front. The infantry deployed into line to the left, facing the enemy's right wing, which, as we have noticed, curved round so as to directly menace the flank of the original line of advance. The infantry therefore stood deployed along the line of the road, facing west, with the guns on their right flank, facing north. One and a half squadrons of the 19th Bengal Lancers stood protecting the left flank of the Infantry. The 2nd Punjab Cavalry were on the right of the guns, whose escort consisted of one squadron 19th Bengal Lancers and one company 19th Punjab Infantry.

The heavy guns were unlimbered on a knoll close to the road, on the extreme left of the line, between them and the 19th Bengal Lancers being a considerable gap. Behind the knoll on which the heavy guns were posted were placed the equipment of the sapper companies and the infantry entrenching tools. The 19th Punjab Infantry, and the Sappers who were in reserve, stood in rear of the left flank.

It was the General's intention to advance to the attack, but at 9 a.m., before his dispositions were fully developed, the whole crest of the curved line of hills held by the enemy was observed to be swarming with men along a front of nearly two miles.

Scarcely had the guns opened fire when from the enemy's position rushed out successive waves of swordsmen on foot, stretching out beyond either flank and seeming to envelop the British force. At the same time a large body of horse rode along the hills, threatening the left flank and rear. As the swordsmen swept down on the Infantry and guns, the Afghan horse poured along two ravines which issued from the hills, and in one mass charged the Lancers before they could acquire sufficient speed to meet them fairly. The Lancers were forced back to their right rear, disordering the 3rd Gurkhas, who were the left battalion of the line. Colonel H. Lyster, V.C., promptly formed his men into company squares, and the Gurkhas stood their ground, but the Lancers were in great confusion, and could not be rallied until they had passed along almost the whole rear of the infantry.

Meantime the swordsmen on foot pressed their attack with fanatical fury, and it was necessary to place the whole reserve in the fighting line. Thus half a battalion of the 19th Punjab Infantry and the Sappers were brought up on the left of the Gurkhas, and the other half battalion, with the two companies of the General's escort, were pushed in between the 59th Foot, which was the right flank battalion, and the two batteries of Artillery on the right.

These two batteries were now firing case shot at close ranges into the swarm of Afghans, but neither this nor the heavy fire from the breechloaders of the infantry could stop the rush of the Gházis. The batteries having expended all their case shot, were compelled to retire about two hundred yards, and the right of the infantry line was also forced back.

At this moment the situation was most critical, for both flanks of the extended line were turned, and the troops were somewhat shaken by the suddenness and vehemence of the attack. The enemy's horsemen, pushing round the left flank, were, however, checked by the firmness of the 3rd Gurkhas and by some well-directed shells from the 40-pounder guns. On the right the 2nd Punjab Cavalry charged and drove back the enemy, enabling the batteries of artillery, whose gallantry and discipline at this trying moment were conspicuous, to take fresh positions and again open fire. The infantry of the right also recovering from the confusion into which they had been momentarily thrown, poured a withering fire into the Afghans. In the centre the 2nd Sikhs had throughout the fight, now in line and now in company squares, maintained their position with unwavering steadiness.

Two guns of the field battery were now moved from the right flank to the left centre, and were followed shortly after by the rest of that battery. Two squadrons of the 1st Punjab Cavalry having now arrived from the rear guard, were, with the 19th Bengal Lancers, pushed out to the right towards the Ghazni River.

By this time the steady and well-directed fire of the whole line, with the battery in its midst, was working fearful havoc amongst the enemy, whose attack was being made clear in the open. After an hour's gallant and strenuous exertion to break the British line, the efforts of the enemy began to fail under the murderous fire. The onslaught was checked, hesitated, and died away, the entire body dispersing broadcast over the country, completely defeated and scattered. The cease fire was sounded at 10 a.m. No cavalry pursuit was ordered owing to the necessity for protecting the large parks and baggage.

The enemy left 1,000 dead on the field, and their total loss amounted to about 3,000. The British loss was only 141, including killed and wounded; of these, 9 were British officers.

We have here a battle very similar in many of its aspects to the battle of Maiwand,* the difference being due to superior *moral* as well perhaps as to superior fighting material on the British side, but which had a very different result. The formations of the British force on both occasions were much the same, and the enemy's tactics were also practically the same.

The battle of Ahmed Kheyl was fought in April, and that of Maiwand in July of the same year. It is quite possible, therefore, that General Burrows, who commanded in the latter battle, made his dispositions to coincide with those that had proved successful in the earlier battle. But it will be noticed that the circumtances were not identical. Sir Donald Stewart had formed up his brigade for attack, and was presumably merely waiting for the arrival of the reinforcements which he had called up before opening the battle. He was, however, forestalled and had to meet a sudden attack, and to act on the defensive in a formation by no means well adapted to stand an enveloping onslaught. It is therefore highly improbable that if he had to fight the battle again he would do so in the

* *Vide* p. 108.

same formation. The experience of these two battles would seem to point in the same direction, that when advancing in the open to attack an enemy who may deliver a counter-charge before the attack is delivered, it is safer to assume some other formation than that of line entire with a small reserve. Undoubtedly the line entire brings at once the largest possible number of rifles to bear on the advancing enemy, but practically the result is to assist rather than check the flow of warriors to both flanks. And these, as they advance, finding that they have passed the most dangerous zone, pour freely on to the flanks and rear of the line. The general tendency of a line at this juncture would be to bend back on both flanks in self-defence, and a brisk attack by the enemy at this moment is very apt to roll up the line, as it succeeded in doing at Maiwand, and very nearly did at Ahmed Kheyl.

A brigade in square is a cumbersome and unwieldy body, and gives at once an appearance of lack of self-confidence, and demonstrates an undue respect for the enemy, thereby tending to vastly encourage them.* A square, therefore, though it is undoubtedly safe, is not to be recommended unless the troops are much shaken by previous defeats, or in cases where other exceptional circumstances dictate clearly the wisdom of having resort to such an expedient. It will probably be found that in a similar battle—and many such may recur against similar foes—that it is wiser to

* The Egyptian Army formation, the battalion of six companies (four in the first line, two in support), would appear to be as near an approach to the ideal as possible. For while giving a good field of fire, if the flank companies are wheeled back, a square is formed for defensive purposes. —[ED.]

diminish the front and to add to the strength of the flanks, whilst Cavalry protects the rear. It would seem more judicious, too, to mass the guns in the centre of the front line rather than to post them on the flanks, detaching such guns as may be required from time to time to assist either flank. Thus a force, consisting of three battalions of Infantry, two batteries, and a regiment of Cavalry, might advantageously be drawn up in line of battle as follows.

The two batteries in the front line flanked on each side by one regiment. Each of these regiments to have one wing in line and aligned with the guns, and the other wing in column of companies immediately in rear of the exposed flank of its own regiment, ready to wheel outwards and form a flank. The third battalion of the brigade being posted in quarter column about 200 yards in rear of the guns, as a reserve. The Cavalry in mass in rear of the reserve.

The happy inspiration of Colonel Lyster in ordering his men to form company squares, an example followed by the 2nd Sikhs in the centre, undoubtedly saved the battle on that flank and the centre. The experience thus gained may well be applied in the future, not only against Cavalry, but against fanatical swordsmen on foot, who are practically, though perhaps not theoretically, quite as dangerous as if mounted on horseback.

It will be noticed that consideration for the safety of the military trains decided the General not to send the Cavalry in pursuit. The experience gained at this battle, as well as at Sherpur, and at the battle of

Kandahar, will give leaders of the future entire confidence on this head. When a force of Afghans is defeated, however bravely it may have fought, it forthwith ceases to exist, and any danger that may up to the moment of defeat have threatened the baggage and trains entirely disappears. In a few hours the whole surrounding country is absolutely deserted, except perhaps for a few harmless-looking villagers. A general may therefore, with perfect confidence, launch every available man and horse in pursuit, and the more promptly this is done the better, for verily the earth seems to swallow up a defeated army of Afghans.

DEFENSIVE.

A long and brilliant series of victories, won generally against great odds, has possibly filled the Indian Army with an overwhelming sense of its own invincibility. Without wishing for a moment to diminish that fine feeling of self-confidence which has helped to win many a battle, it is only wise to examine in a critical spirit the reverse of the medal. For the student will learn perhaps as much from reverses as from victories, and by balancing the accounts of both, learn to appreciate how narrow a margin divides one from the other.

THE BATTLE OF MAIWAND.

The most important and decisive defeat which the Indian Army has suffered on the confines of India during late years, fell upon a mixed brigade of British and Bombay troops during the Afghan War, 1878-80, at Maiwand, a village some fifty miles north-west of Kandahar.

During the early days of July, 1880, certain information reached Kandahar that a considerable demonstration was being made from the direction of Herat by a few thousand men under Ayoub Khan. The original object of the demonstration appears to have been not against Kandahar itself, but rather, leaving it severely alone, to penetrate by a bye-route to Ghazni, and there raise the standard of revolt. To intercept this movement a brigade of a total strength of 2,599 men, of which 565 were cavalry, and 12 guns, six of which were captured smooth-bores, under Brigadier-General Burrows, was despatched from Kandahar, and after various movements, which it is not necessary here to discuss, found itself entrenched at Khushk-i-Nakhud on July 26th.

On this night information was received to the effect that the village of Maiwand, which was distant about eleven miles, had been occupied by the advanced irregular troops of the enemy, supported by a body of cavalry some three miles in rear.

General Burrows decided to march at dawn and to attack these troops. After considerable delay owing to the unwieldiness of the transport train, the brigade was put in motion, marching over the perfectly open plain in line of columns of companies with cavalry patrols thrown out on all sides. At 10 a.m. a spy brought in certain information that Ayoub Khan was holding Maiwand in force, and soon afterwards the vedettes saw large bodies of troops about six miles ahead, moving towards that place. The general direction of the enemy's march was obliquely across the front of the British force, and Ayoub Khan was probably quite unaware up to this moment of its advance from Khushk-i-Nakhud. To manœuvre his line of columns so that they should, as he calculated, head in the right direction, General Burrows changed direction three-quarters left, but during the movement came across a large nullah, which somewhat broke his formation, and much fatigued the outside regiment. Issuing from this nullah the brigade deployed into line, the 1st Bombay Grenadiers being on the left, the right wing of the 30th Bombay Infantry (Jacob's Rifles) in the centre, and the 66th Foot on the right, whilst in support, and from 200 to 300 yards in rear of the centre, were one company of Sappers, and the left wing of Jacob's Rifles. After advancing a short distance in this order, the brigade was ordered to halt and lie down. Meanwhile the Artillery, which consisted of one battery of Horse Artillery and one battery of captui smooth-bores, after galloping forward and driving off the enemy's cavalry, was called in and was formed up in échelon of sections, the whole mass being to the left and some 500 yards in front of the infantry line. The escort to the guns consisted of two squadrons of the 3rd Bombay Cavalry, and one troop of the 3rd Sind Horse. The field hospital was established in the nullah to the rear of the Infantry, and here also was parked the greater part of the baggage. In rear of the baggage were two squadrons of

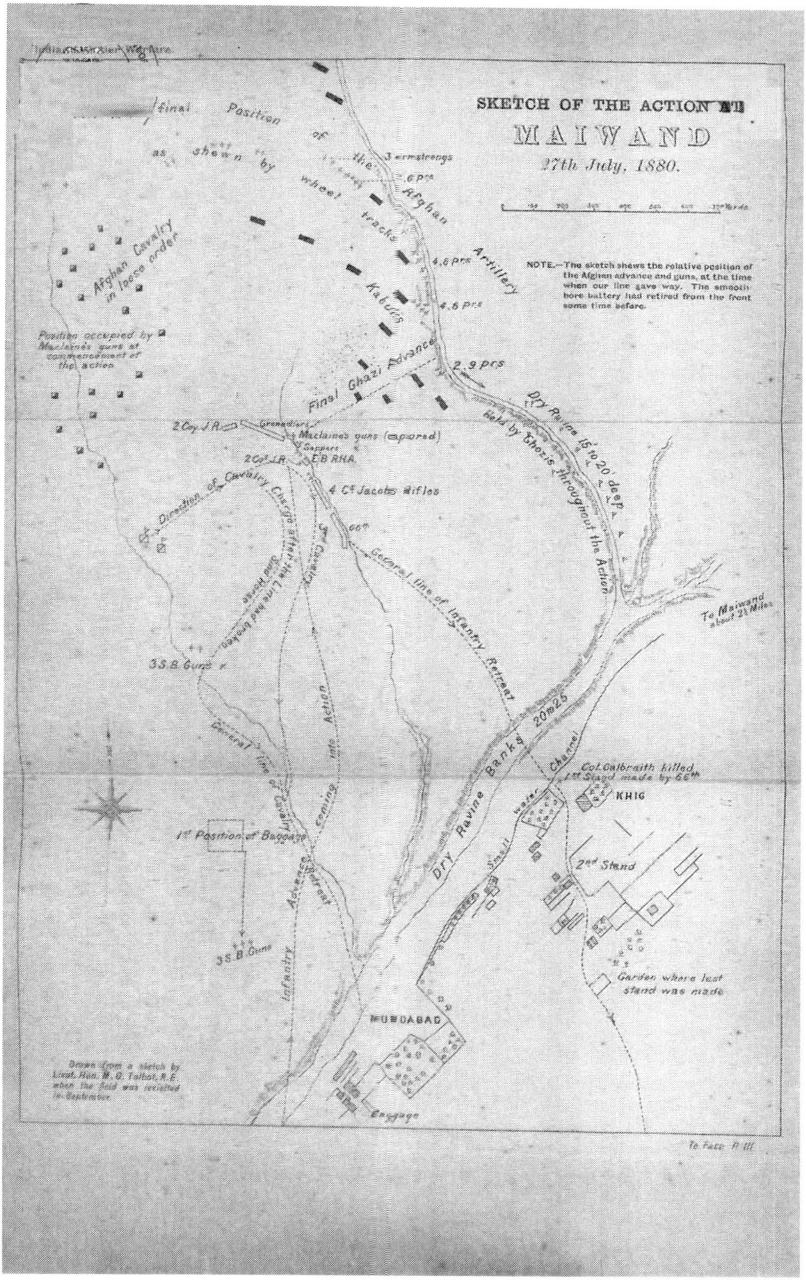
Indian Frontier Warfare.
SKETCH OF THE ACTION AT
MAIWAND
27th July, 1880.
NOTE.—The sketch shews the relative position of the Afghan advance and guns, at the time when our line gave way. The smooth-bore battery had retired from the front some time before.
final Position of the Afghan Artillery as shewn by wheel tracks
3 armstrongs
6 Prs
4.6 Prs
4.6 Prs
2.9 prs
Afghan Cavalry in loose order
Kabulis
Position occupied by Maclaine's guns at commencement of the action
Final Ghazi Advance
Dry Ravine 15' to 20' deep held by Ghazis throughout the Action
2 Coy. J.R.
Grenadiers
Maclaine's guns (captured)
Sappers
2 Coy. J.R.
E.B. R.H.A.
4 Cos. Jacobs Rifles
66th
Direction of Cavalry Charge after the Line had broken
Sind Horse
3rd Cavalry
General line of Infantry Retreat
To Maiwand about 2½ Miles
3 S.B. Guns
General line of Cavalry
coming into Action
Dry Ravine Banks 20 to 25
Small Water Channel
Col. Galbraith killed
1st Stand made by 66th
KHIG
2nd Stand
1st Position of Baggage
Infantry Advance
Retreat
3 S.B. Guns
Garden where last stand was made
MUNDABAD
Baggage
Drawn from a sketch by Lieut. Hon. M. G. Talbot, R.E. when the field was revisited in September
To Face P. 111

the 3rd Sind Horse, which had during the march acted as a rear guard.

At 10.50 a.m. the enemy's artillery came into action, and crowds of Gházis were seen swarming round to the right of the British line, whilst large bodies of Herati and irregular horsemen circled round the left flank of the British, threatening even the rear-guard squadrons. The British force remained stationary, and the enemy, encouraged by this inaction, wheeled his regular infantry into line, facing it and hurrying up more guns from the rear, brought them successively into action, some taking position on the right and others on the left, small nullahs and depressions in the ground covering their advance.

A heavy artillery duel, sustained by both sides with great vigour, now commenced, and under cover of it the British line of Infantry was advanced 500 yards, bringing it up more or less abreast of its own guns, but with its distribution considerably altered. Thus taken from right to left the brigade stood in line as follows. On the right the 66th Foot, and next it one wing of Jacob's Rifles. Then came two guns Royal Horse Artillery, then two companies Jacob's Rifles, then two more guns Royal Horse Artillery, next one company Sappers, then two more guns Royal Horse Artillery, then the 1st Bombay Grenadiers with the smooth-bore guns, whilst on the extreme left flank of the line were two companies of Jacob's Rifles. There were apparently no troops in support or reserve. The Cavalry occupied about the same relative position as before. Thus matters stood at 11.15 a.m.

For about one hour the artillery duel continued with increasing vigour on the part of the enemy, whose superior strength in guns told heavily At about 12.15 noon, two of the smooth-bore guns were moved to the right of the 66th Foot as the enemy's attack began to develop in that direction, whilst the fire of the howitzers (part of the smooth-bore battery) was directed against the Herati cavalry, who were threatening the left. This left flank was further strengthened by fifty sabres of the 3rd Sind Horse. The pressure of the enemy on both flanks at this period became so heavy that the British line gradually took the form of a horseshoe with both flanks thrown back. At the same time the rear guard and baggage guard were hotly engaged with the enemy, who now surrounded the force on every side. Still using the protection of a favouring nullah, the enemy now ran his guns up to within 700 yards, and, together with a number of riflemen, took the British batteries in flank and handled them very severely. The enemy had altogether six breechloading 9-pounder Armstrong guns, sixteen M.L. S.B. 6-pounder guns, and two S.B. 12-pounder howitzers, also two mountain howitzers, 4⅗-inch, and four 3-pounder guns—total thirty pieces of ordnance.

Soon after 1.30 p.m. the British smooth-bore battery ran out of ammunition, and had to be sent to the rear to replenish. Up to this time the Infantry, who had been lying down, had not suffered much, the 66th Foot firing steady volleys by companies at the gun detachments and dense masses of the enemy. But now affairs took a critical turn, for not only had the enemy successfully planted four 9-pounder Armstrong guns within 700 yards, but had also managed to push another battery up to within 500 yards on that flank, and finally planted two 3-pounder mountain guns directly opposite the centre of the British line and within 500 yards of it. At the same time the regular Kabuli and Herati infantry regiments advanced in successive lines, all apparently more or less under cover, whilst crowds of Ghazis planted their standards within 700 yards to the front of the 66th Foot, and poured down the side ravines to their right and right rear. The retirement of the smooth-bores to replenish ammunition came, it would appear, at an unfortunate moment, for up to now the British, though hard pressed, were standing firm.

From this time onwards, disaster followed disaster. The Ghazis to the right rear of the 66th Foot were now seen boldly pressing forward sword in hand, and all the attempts of their officers failed to induce the 3rd Sind Horse* to charge and stave off the rush. Jacob's Rifles and the Sappers kept up a heavy fire on the enemy, attacking in front whilst the 1st Bombay Grenadiers and the two companies of Jacob's Rifles on the left were keeping up a more or less effective fusillade. The Afghan cavalry, the Ghazis and Kabuli infantry, now again advanced on the British left flank and left front, the two flank companies of Jacob's

* It may be noted that the 3rd Sind Horse, and the remnants of Jacob's Rifles, were afterwards disbanded, and, together with the 1st Bombay Grenadiers, thoroughly reconstituted.

Rifles giving way before them. The Horse Artillery guns, being now in great danger, were ordered to limber up and retire, but two of them which were served till the Ghazis were within twenty yards of their muzzles fell into the enemy's hands. The rest of the battery with the smooth-bores crossed the big nullah in rear of the British position and came again into action.

Between 2 p.m. and 3 p.m., the fire of the enemy's guns began to slacken and hopes were entertained that his ammunition was running short, but it became immediately apparent that the cessation was merely to allow of a grand attack of the Ghazis. This attack, in spite of the heavy fire, was successful, the Grenadiers and the remainder of Jacob's Rifles being rolled up from left to right on to the 66th Foot. This regiment thus pressed by the Ghazis in front, and by the broken sepoys on their left and rear, retired to their right rear, still preserving cohesion, the men turning round to deliver their fire into the crowd of Afghans who were within 25 yards, and eventually crossed the great nullah in rear. To give the infantry time to reform, General Burrows now ordered a cavalry charge, but this was made in so half-hearted a manner as to be practically useless. Henceforth, the defeat became a rout, which need not be described.

The British losses were, in killed and wounded, 1,109 men, including 29 officers, as well as 338 camp followers, and 269 horses. The number of troops actually engaged was 2,476.

The battle of Maiwand, like many of those which

occur at the commencement of a campaign, or which open a new phase of a campaign, was, on both sides, what may be termed a chance encounter.

General Burrows relinquished a position at Khushk-i-Nakhud, where he had halted, strongly entrenched, for several days, for the purpose of attacking and dispersing a small body of Ghazis and cavalry reported to be in the vicinity of Maiwand, whilst Ayoub Khan, entirely ignorant of General Burrows' advance, was marching across his front, and had not the least expectation of meeting him. On such small matters do the fate of battles hang that it is quite open to conjecture whether the two armies would not have entirely missed each other if General Burrows had started at dawn as he had intended, for the tracks of the two forces, if prolonged, cross each other. Or had he started later, the spy carrying the information of Ayoub Khan's whereabouts would have reached him in time to stop his march. It may seem improbable that two forces of considerable strength should miss each other in a perfectly open and level country, but, as a matter of fact, the heat-haze and mirage made objects so indistinct that even with field-glasses the officers with the advanced squadrons of Burrows' force were for some time doubtful whether the enemy were clumps of trees or merely cattle grazing. Haze and mirage can not only efface all trace of a force, but, as is well known, substantial villages and lakes of water are made to appear where none exist.

Though Ayoub Khan's force was immensely superior in guns and in numbers to the British, for the comparative strength was probably ten to one in his favour, yet a British force, in good fettle and well handled, has won many a victory against equal odds. It is apparent therefore that we must look to causes apart from actual aptitude for battle to account for Ayoub Khan's victory. These are not difficult to find. In the first place the day was in the month of July, one of the hottest in the year, and as the day advanced, every step the troops took forward found the power of the sun increasing, till the heat became intense. To a solitary traveller on foot, marching in such a temperature, the task would be an arduous one, much more so to a soldier marching heavily loaded and formed up in column of companies, which it is generally allowed is one of the most fatiguing formations for a prolonged advance. The 66th Foot, before starting, had been served out with tea and a light breakfast, but the native troops had had nothing to eat since the night before. One regiment, the 1st Bombay Grenadiers, had no water to drink, but the rest managed to fill their water bottles during a halt which lasted from 8.30 to 9.15. Already a good deal fatigued on account of the heat and mode of marching, the brigade at the end of it, that is, just before the battle began, were ordered to change front three-quarters left. During this movement the Grenadiers, the pivot regiment (the brigade being in line of battalion columns), did not slacken its pace to any appreciable extent, consequently the centre and outer flank regiments became greatly exhausted in trying to keep in place during the wheel.

The whole brigade, therefore, arrived hungry, thirsty, and much exhausted, to take part in a battle which was fought at midday, under a tropical sun, and at the hottest period of the year.

When the two belligerents first came into contact, there was no appreciable advantage of ground on either side. But General Burrows' advance, as if a hideous fatality pursued it, brought his line into such a position that behind him lay a great nullah, whilst other nullahs and depressions in the ground so ran into his position that during the course of the battle the enemy were enabled to bring guns up to within 700 yards, and latterly to within 500 yards of his front and flanks. Indeed, it was remarked by General Daubeny, who a month later was sent to inspect the ground, that the wheel marks of the enemy's artillery showed that they had been at closer ranges during the battle than the British had any conception of. General Burrows explains that he moved forward into the position he finally took up to support the guns, which, by galloping forward and opening fire nearly two miles ahead, had precipitated the battle.

Allowing that such was the motive on this occasion, it would be hardly permissible to uphold the principle that the plans of a general are dependent on the, perhaps, irresponsible action of a few guns. The mistake made on this occasion is sufficiently apparent to those judging after the event, but the initial cause lies deeper than in the error of judgment of one general. As long as we as soldiers, and the public educated through us, continue to lay fictitious value on a gun as such, so long will leaders be led into incurring unnecessary risks to support or save guns. The sentiment originated in the days when guns were few and costly, and the lack of roads and means of transit had made them difficult to replace.

The loss of a gun therefore at that era was a material loss to one side and a material gain to the other. At the present day, and more especially when fighting against the foes we meet on the frontiers of India, the loss of a gun, apart from the fictitious sentiment that surrounds it, is practically of no consequence. We have hundreds more of like pattern in our arsenals to replace it, and the enemy have neither the ammunition nor the skill to use it. Yet some generals' hands still seem tied by this sentiment; they may win the most brilliant victory, but the loss of a single gun is held to completely dim it.

It will be noticed that when the British brigade advanced to its second position, it formed up in line entire, without supports or reserve, both flanks being practically *en l'air*. If any proof were required that this is an essentially weak formation, it is furnished by the fact that the line was almost immediately bent back on both flanks, till latterly the general formation of the brigade became that of a horseshoe. There is little doubt that even the best troops, be they British or native, are apt to recoil before the determined rush of dense masses of a fanatical foe. The best and most seasoned troops are indeed capable of the moral courage of standing this rush, formed up in line entire, and of repulsing it; but with any but the best, or with troops new to these tactics, some more solid formation is required to stand the shock—that shock, be it understood, being more moral than physical. There can be no shadow of a doubt that the rush of the Ghazis at the battle of Ahmed Kheyl* was withstood and driven off by the presence of mind of the commanding officers, who formed their men into company squares. To form squares or groups, of some sort, where the men get the moral support of being back to back with their comrades, is a recognized formation for meeting an attack of cavalry. The rush of Ghazis is practically the charge of dismounted swordsmen, who, though not travelling as fast as cavalry, yet move at a great pace, with considerable cohesion and with great hardihood. It would seem wise therefore not to run the risk, as a rule, of meeting such a rush in line.

With regard to the two cavalry regiments belonging to the British force, the account of the battle sufficiently demonstrates that they can hardly be held to have distinguished themselves. That, however, was probably due to deficiency in *moral* and lack of good fighting material in the ranks, matters which have since been reformed, and therefore need not be further alluded to. But one point, which comes out as a side light, has an interesting bearing on the question of the use of firearms by cavalry. Unimpeachable eye-witnesses state officially that the 3rd Sind Horse when called on to charge were found with their carbines drawn instead of their swords, that

* *Vide* p. 103.

they returned carbines and drew swords with the greatest reluctance, and that shortly after, when again called upon to charge, it was found that they had again returned swords and taken out their carbines. The natural deduction is that the men of this regiment had been trained to place more confidence in their carbines than in their swords, so much so that instinctively, even when mounted, and not required to use them, they drew their carbines in preference to their swords. This is one more proof of the dictum that cavalry who are habituated to rely on their firearms are apt to lose their distinctive characteristics of promptitude, impulsion, and resolution.

That the defeat was chiefly owing to moral causes may be gathered from such deductions as we are in a position to make. Direct evidence of a reliable nature is difficult to get, for even after a victory no two versions of a battle completely agree, much less do they do so after the turmoil of a defeat. Undoubtedly the artillery lost heavily in horses, and possibly in men, though only one officer* was wounded during the battle. The batteries probably formed the conspicuous target on which the fire of the enemy, both artillery and infantry, was concentrated; and in the same way those portions of the infantry which were nearest the guns probably fell in for a goodly share of shot and shell aimed at the battery. But, on the other hand, not a single officer of either of the cavalry regiments was killed, and only one was wounded, though, being mounted, the cavalry was naturally much exposed.

* Another officer was killed during the retirement.

Nor does it appear that any officers of the 66th Foot were killed or wounded until the line broke. Jacob's Rifles lost two officers killed in the fighting line, and the Grenadiers apparently lost no officers before breaking. Taking the general run of battles in the East, the proportion of officers to men killed is always abnormally large, and applying such a percentage to the battle of Maiwand, it is only possible to come to the conclusion that the loss amongst the men was very small until the line broke. Truly in the day of battle the moral is to the physical as three to one. This is probably the great lesson to be learnt from this engagement, and if such a lesson be laid to heart, the bitter experiences of the day, though dearly bought, will not have been bought in vain.

NOTE.—A possible explanation of the carbine incident is to be found in the fact that the Sind Horse were originally armed with double-barrelled carbines, the invention of General Jacob. Now this brilliant frontier leader was the very last man to have believed in cavalry using a firearm when mounted. But he had originally raised his men to act "indifferently" on horse or foot, and a possible result is that in either case they were indifferent.—ED.

CHAPTER V.

Minor Operations.

Very instructive, and more especially so to the young officer, are the instances where detachments and small bodies of troops have been called upon, often at a moment's notice, to undertake offensive operations in different portions of the Indian frontier.

For many years after our acquisition of the Punjab and the consequent advance of our frontiers to their present limits, the difficulty of concentrating troops without railways, the danger of leaving portions of the frontier unguarded to reinforce others, and the generally accepted notion that a blow received must, to be effective, be at once returned, led to a general adoption of the raid and counter-raid form of warfare, using only the troops actually at hand and available for the enterprise. To keen soldiers who as subalterns commanded regiments, the system had many attractions. A certain portion of the frontier was placed in charge of each, and the cattle raiding, armed outrages, and border ruffianism were met with the short, sharp counter-blows of hardy little bodies of troops, ready for action at a moment's notice. But as time went on it was found that, though each little affair might be brilliantly successful, yet that the general result, in so far as arriving at a more settled condition of affairs on the frontier generally, was wanting. The punishment inflicted was local and easily forgotten: a few men killed, a few cattle lost, and a few mud huts destroyed. The tribesmen were accustomed to lose as much, and sometimes more, in the constantly recurring village disputes which took place amongst themselves. It soon, therefore, began to force itself on the attention of the authorities that operations on a larger scale—of such magnitude, in fact, as to give a serious lesson to those in need of it—must replace the old system. The enormous extension of the Indian railway system removed the difficulty regarding concentrations and guarding denuded portions of the frontier, and paved the way for the systematic introduction of the modern system. But although it has become an almost established principle that offences on the frontier shall be punished on an extensive scale, yet it may any day happen that urgent necessity may require the immediate use in small bodies of local troops. It is, therefore, proposed to give a few examples of how such operations have been conducted in the past, and later to ask the reader's indulgence whilst conclusions are drawn as to the best method of applying the experience of the past to the possibilities of the future.

Small parties of troops have, as a rule, been employed either to support the authority of the civil power, to protect a suddenly threatened village, to follow up marauders or cattle-lifters hotfoot, occasionally to arrest an important outlaw, known to be harboured in a trans-border village, and sometimes to attack in form mountain fastnesses.

In most cases of warfare on a more important scale, secrecy, both in the preparation and in the execution of an operation, is very essential. In the form of fighting with which we are now dealing it is absolutely imperative. Even when the operation merely aims at covering a threatened village, secrecy is most important. For though it may appear at first sight that publicity and show of force rather than secrecy would best serve the purpose, yet it has been found by experience that the most effective way of protecting a friendly village, and at the same time inculcating a wholesome lesson for the future, is to allow the enemy, however astute, to boldly attack that village, in the confidence that he has only half-armed and undisciplined villagers to deal with, finding only too late that he is committed to the attack on a village garrisoned by two or three hundred seasoned troops, armed with breech-loaders. If in such a case secrecy is required, much more so is it necessary when the object of the enterprise is to surprise a trans-border village, or to forcibly capture an outlaw in the enemy's country. To maintain secrecy in a country where news proverbially flies on the wings of the wind is in itself a most difficult task. To order supplies, or to collect transport, would at once give notice to ever watchful eyes that something was astir, and the expedition would be doomed to failure before it started. It is therefore necessary to plan such an affair so as to allow of its execution with the means actually at hand and without collecting supplies or transport. As has before been mentioned, as a general rule such minor operations extend merely to a matter of hours, so that the question of supplies is not usually a weighty one; whilst, as to transport, a small nucleus of baggage animals is kept up permanently at all frontier stations, and these could be utilized for the occasion. When, however, the troops must be absent for more than twenty-four hours, the question of supply would naturally arise.

The usual plan, under such circumstances, supposing always that the enemy's country affords no supplies, is to leave orders, to be opened after the troops have started, directing that provisions when collected should follow the route taken, so as to meet the force on its return journey; or it may be feasible to direct the formation of a supply depôt at some given point, which the troops, having made a detour, would pass as they work homewards.

It will be apparent, however, to the military student that, however carefully the secret may have been kept up to the moment of departure, yet that the moment the troops make a move along any particular road good grounds are afforded to the whole country-side for guessing what their ultimate destination is likely to be. This clue once given, the surprise would be foredoomed to failure, for fleet runners and riders would carry ample warning to the enemy. It is therefore necessary, where strict secrecy is required, to move at night, so timing the hour of departure as to start without attracting attention.

Next to secrecy, the most important factor in the success of one of these raids, or small expeditions, is rapidity. And it is not only imperative to reach the objective point with rapidity, but circumstances may make it necessary for the return march to be equally rapid. For though the force employed may be strong enough to effect its purpose, yet it may not be strong enough to hold its own when the tribesmen begin to concentrate, as they assuredly would on hearing that a small force was deeply committed in the intricacies of their country. If the force used consists entirely of cavalry rapidity can be ensured; but it is rarely possible for cavalry alone to manage the undertaking, though instances will be quoted where they have done so with the greatest success. It is more usual, however, to employ infantry, with or without the aid of mountain guns, and as it is not fair to ask even the best infantry to cover at a stretch more than thirty miles at an average rate of from two and a half to two and three-quarter miles an hour, it becomes necessary to afford them some assistance.

It will therefore generally be found necessary to accelerate the march of the infantry by using such means of transporting them as may be at hand. Thus pack mules and ponies, or ekkas, the two-wheeled pony carts of the country, are generally available. In this way, by using the country pack-saddle, a mule or stout pony would carry two infantrymen, and moving at the native ambling pace would cover four and a half to five miles an hour, whilst animals with the Government pack-saddle would each carry one rider. An ekka is capable of carrying three men besides the driver. Thus starting in secrecy and moving thus rapidly, the two main elements in a successful undertaking of this nature are secured. Ceasing for the moment from dealing with this subject in the abstract, let us proceed to illustrate the general axioms put forth by referring to some of the most successful undertakings of this nature which have been recorded. The examples given will deal mostly with recent times, that is, with operations undertaken since the introduction of breech-loaders; but occasionally some older raids, where lessons unconnected with the improvement in firearms are to be learnt, may find a place.

Amongst the greatest and most successful of the school of frontier officials who in recent times have used small bodies of troops to back up the civil power may be reckoned the name of Sir Louis Cavagnari, the same officer who was afterwards murdered whilst British Envoy at Kabul. Cavagnari worked mainly on that principle of reprisals which has already been alluded to. His principle was first to place a heavy, but just, fine upon the village responsible for a breach of the peace, and if it was not paid within a prescribed period to bring matters to a climax by making a sudden descent, with a body of picked troops at his back. He thus aimed at instilling a becoming respect for international amenities and an abiding sense of the ubiquity and far-reaching power of the British Government. Amongst many which he undertook, perhaps one of the most successful and instructive of these sudden raids is furnished by the surprise of the village of Sappri, in 1878.

The village of Sappri lies about seven miles across

the border, not far distant from Peshawur and close to the spot where the Swat River issues from the border mountains. During the year 1877 a new canal, which follows the line of an ancient Bhuddist cutting, was being constructed by the Government to tap the Swat River at the point where it enters British territory. The ignorant trans-border tribesmen, always suspicious, saw here, in their ignorance, a deeply-laid British plot, which, under the guise of an engineering project, in reality threatened their dearly-treasured independence. As a vigorous protest, therefore, a body of desperadoes descended upon the canal works and in cold blood murdered a large number of the inoffensive coolies employed upon the work of excavation. On enquiry, it was found that the instigator and principal agent in this cruel and dastardly outrage was the Khan of the neighbouring trans-border village of Sappri. Cavagnari immediately ordered this chief to pay a heavy fine in money and cattle, and in addition directed him to hand over the actual murderers, to be tried for their crime in a British court of justice. The Khan took no notice of either the fine or of the demand, and Cavagnari, with his customary promptitude, prepared for stronger measures.

Lying some forty miles by road south-east of Sappri is the British cantonment of Murdan, where the corps of Guides is permanently quartered. The greater part of the corps, which consists of cavalry and infantry, was, at this time, absent on another expedition, but there remained present and available for use two squadrons of cavalry and eleven rifles. This small force Cavagnari determined to use for the purpose he had in hand.

To the officer commanding only, the brave and gallant Captain Wigram Battye, who was afterwards killed in Afghanistan, did Cavagnari give the slightest hint of his intentions. Indeed, so profoundly was the secret kept, that the officers, unaware of any contemplated move, were playing a game of raquets when called upon to prepare to start. To the men not a word of warning was given, but at evening roll-call the fort gates were closed so that no one could go in or out, and ball-ammunition was served out to all. To old soldiers who had been on many a raid before an extra packet or two of ball-ammunition meant fighting, and at sight of it a great shout went up, which shout was indeed the first intimation that the junior officers had that anything was astir.

The infantrymen were supplied with mules, the order to mount was given, and the small force, consisting of 255 sabres and 11 rifles, set off on its long night march. The rate of march was naturally regulated by the pace of the infantry on mules, but these, being picked animals and in good condition, covered more than four miles an hour. After marching for seven hours, and after having covered 32 miles, with only one or two brief halts, the force reached the British frontier fort of Abazai, which lies about seven miles south of Sappri. The country onwards being impracticable for cavalry, all the horses and mules were left at Abazai, and the party, now consisting of 212 men, of whom the majority were dismounted cavalrymen, proceeded on foot into the hills. After seven miles severe marching the near vicinity of the hostile village was reached. Silently, and with the utmost caution, Captain Battye placed his men on the surrounding high ground, so as to completely command the village and every exit from it. Just as his dispositions were completed without arousing the enemy, the day broke.

With the dawn Cavagnari sent in a formal demand to the Khan to surrender the outlaws and to pay the fine due from the village. The Khan, though completely surprised, refused to comply with the terms demanded. A short but desperate fight took place, in which the Guides were victorious. The Khan and several of his leading men were killed and the village captured. The fine was then exacted, and the troops marched back to Fort Abazai. In this raid the Guides covered 48 miles without a halt, and fought a stiff fight against very superior numbers.

In this case we have exemplified those elements necessary for the execution of a successful frontier raid. We have secrecy, rapidity, and a vigorous offensive. We have troops ready to move off at a moment's notice, horses and men trained to undergo unusual labour without special preparation, cavalry ready to perform on emergency the *rôle* of infantry, and infantry prepared on occasion to ride thirty miles with cavalry.

The question of supplies was, on this occasion, easily settled; the friendly villages round Fort Abazai furnished all that was required on the return of the troops. Transport animals, save for mounting the party of infantry, were not required.

It must be conceded, however, that for one completely successful surprise there are many unsuccessful enterprises. Nor is this to be wondered at when we consider the animal sagacity which appears to warn a semi-barbarian of approaching danger. As showing how easily matters may go wrong, and how difficult it is even with the most carefully laid plans, to ensure the accuracy of night operations which aim at surprise, we may quote the instance of Malandrai.

The cause of strife was a common one. A series of cattle-lifting raids and counter-raids had for some weeks been carried on between hostile villages, standing a couple of miles or so across the border on the one side, and the village of Rustam, which is in British territory, on the other side. Whilst this state of hostility existed, information was received that several of the most important amongst the enemy's raiders, as well as a goodly head of cattle, might be found on a certain night in the village of Malandrai, which lay about two miles beyond the border. It was decided, therefore, to attempt a cutting-out expedition.

The force available within striking distance was one battalion of the Guides Infantry, and one squadron of the 12th Bengal Cavalry, which were lying at the fort of Mardan, twenty-nine miles from the Malandrai.

The plan of operations was as follows:

Two companies of infantry starting at 2 p.m. were to reach Rustam, 25 miles distant, after darkness had set in. They were here to take a short rest, and were then to continue their way by a circuitous and difficult track through the hills, so timing their march as to appear on a commanding spur in the rear of Malandrai village at dawn, when it was proposed that the frontal attack should take place. The remainder of the infantry, consisting of the six companies who were to execute the frontal attack, were timed to start from Mardan at dusk, and to arrive before Malandrai in the small hours of the morning. The squadron of cavalry, moving independently, was ordered to time its arrival so as to cut off any of the enemy who, escaping from the frontal attack, failed to fall into the hands of the turning party.

The village of Malandrai lies at the foot of a steep, rocky spur, covered with dense brushwood, standing as high as a man. This spur, with many others right and left, runs into a small valley, covered with bushes and boulders, to which the only entrance is a narrow watercourse, dry at that season of the year. It was anticipated that the turning party, working through the hills, would arrive on the spur above the village, and there remain concealed till the frontal attack developed itself. It was known that the enemy had a night piquet in the gorge through which the troops forming the frontal attack must pass, and therefore it was decided that the main body should, if it arrived before the appointed time, halt and lie concealed just short of that point. A selected party was to have stalked and rushed the enemy's piquet at dawn to prevent its giving the alarm.

The turning party of two companies, after a most laborious march of eighteen hours, the greater part of it by night, through terribly rough country, and having often to crawl along on hands and knees for safety, arrived at the appointed spot at dawn. The main body was not so fortunate. In the inky darkness the village guides miscalculated their distance, and instead of halting short of the gorge, the column suddenly stumbled on to the piquets guarding it. The enemy fired a scattered volley, killing the colonel of the regiment and a few of the men, and were now fully warned that something was astir. The surprise therefore, as a surprise, failed, but an attack in form was delivered when daylight came, and the turning party extricated from its precarious position.

We have here one of those instances, an unsuccessful one on this occasion, where the ordinary rules of warfare are knowingly disregarded. Thus we find two companies of infantry launched into the enemy's country without support and committed to one of those wide turning movements which are generally considered unsound. Yet, had it not been for the accidental *rencontre* with the piquet in the gorge the operation would have been completely successful. The turning party was comfortably concealed within 400 yards of the village, and commanding it in a perfectly secure position when day broke, and had the frontal attack taken place as proposed the enemy would have found himself in a *cul-de-sac* hemmed in on every side.

The immense moral effect which guns have in warfare with semi-barbarous tribes, who are themselves deficient in artillery, is very marked. The presence of even a couple of mountain guns, without appreciably affecting the mobility of the force, is of the very greatest advantage to a body of infantry engaged in operations directed against mountain fastnesses. The *rôle* of artillery here, as elsewhere, is to pave the way for the infantry attack; but, on the other hand, it sometimes so happens that, in the attack on fortified positions in mountainous regions, where swamps and thick bush surround them, it is impossible to prepare the way for the infantry advance by artillery fire. The mountain artillery of the Indian Army has learnt to be able to follow infantry over the most difficult ground, but it occasionally happens that the ground is not only impassable for the mules which carry the guns, but even to transport them within striking distance by hand is very difficult. It must be remembered also that the mountain gun, though an excellent weapon, cannot breach solid masonry defences or appreciably damage earthworks. Thus we find that at the storming of Nilt Fort in the Hunza and Nagar Expedition of 1891, though a spur actually commanded the fort at close range, yet it was found perfectly impossible even by hand to get the guns on to it. And even if they had been successfully placed on the spur, the head cover in the fort is reported to have been so strong and so carefully constructed as to be practically impervious to the fire of field guns.

Again, in the course of the Burmah War of 1886-87, we find frequent mention of occasions on which the guns carried by hand in regions impassable for mules could not be brought into action owing to the

ROUGH SKETCH OF NILT FORT.

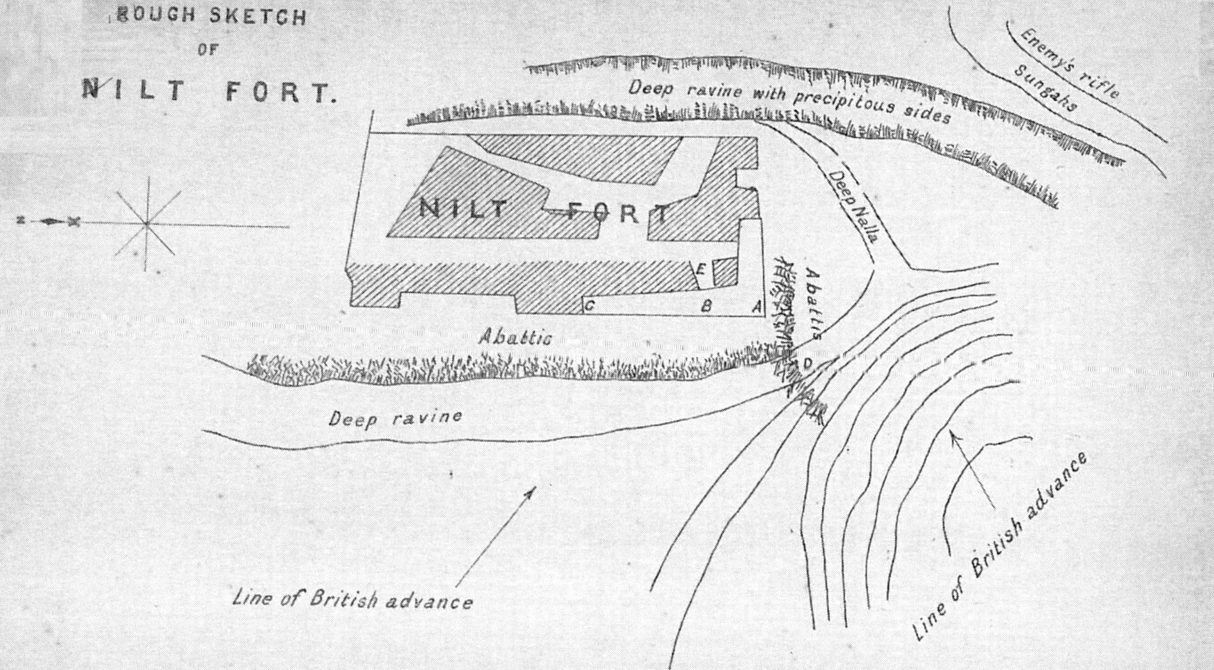

To Face P. 135.

exhaustion of the carriers ; or, having been successfully placed in position, it was found that the thick bush effectually prevented the full use of the weapon.

It will be seen then that occasions occur when it is necessary for the assaulting columns to move to the attack of strong positions, the defenders of which have been unshaken by artillery fire, and on many occasions these assaults have had to take the form of direct frontal attacks. A good instance is afforded by the bold manner in which, in spite of these tremendous disadvantages, the fort of Nilt was assaulted and taken.

THE STORMING OF NILT FORT.

The fort was one of great strength, placed at the junction of two precipitous cliffs several hundred feet high, which form the banks of the Hunza River, and of a great ravine that here runs into it. Owing to the configuration of the ground, the fort could not be properly seen till the force was within 300 yards of it, and no fire to speak of, either from guns or rifles, could be brought to bear on it until within 250 yards. The walls of the fort were of solid stone, cemented by mud, and strengthened by large timbers. They averaged 14 feet in height and 8 feet in thickness, with towers at the angles and in the centres of the faces, affording good flank fire. The head cover throughout the fort was perfect. In front of the main wall ran a loopholed wall (A, B, C), completely hiding the gateway. In front of this again was a very deep ditch, encumbered with abattis, whilst a broad band of abattis (D) filled transversely the space which intervened between the ditch and a precipitous spur from the adjacent mountain. This spur was crowned by our infantry but was inaccessible for guns, and infantry fire was of no avail owing to the good head cover which the enemy had erected. It became imperative, therefore, to make a direct attack and to storm the fort on a front of only sixty yards.

The only possible points of entry were by the two gates at A and B. After a vain attempt to make some impression on the fort with mountain guns, Colonel Durand ordered the infantry attack. The force available amounted to 12 British officers and 1,031 men, of whom 188 belonged to the 5th Gurkhas (the rest being Kashmir troops), together with two mountain guns. On receiving the order to advance, Lieutenants Boisragon and Badcock, with the Gurkhas, and Captain Aylmer, R.E., with a company of sappers, dashed forward into the ravine facing the west wall of the fort. A few of the Gurkhas, with Captain Aylmer and Lieutenant Boisragon, managed to force their way through a weak point in the abattis, under a heavy fire from the fort, and worked round to a point opposite the gateway marked A. Hacking this down, the party burst into the courtyard, and Captain Aylmer at once set to work under a very heavy fire to place a charge of gun-cotton against the main entrance into the fort, marked E. After repeated failures the fuze was lighted and the gate blown in. Captain Aylmer was severely wounded in three places by the fierce fire immediately poured on the party, and several of the men were killed. At this moment a small reinforcement, under Lieutenant Badcock, forced its way in as far as the same point, and Lieutenant Boisragon went back under a very hot fire to collect more men and show them the way in. So far the attack had been so astonishingly bold and quick that our own men even were unaware of the success, and Colonel Durand thought that the explosion caused by the blowing up of the gate was due to the bursting of one of the enemy's guns destroyed by the fire of his own, which were all this while firing steadily into the fort. The position of the little band of twenty men and three officers was indeed precarious, thus exposed to a deadly fire from behind as well as from in front. But with the finest heroism they held on unfalteringly to the advantage gained, till, reinforcements arriving, the storming party pushed home its advantage and the fort was captured.

Here was one of the numerous occasions on which neither tactics nor strategy would have been of avail, the successful result being due to cool and determined leading and a fine disregard of the principle of self-preservation which the introduction of the breech-loader has somewhat tended to increase.

Military operations have often on the frontiers of India to be carried on at high altitudes, and not infrequently in the depth of winter. The physical difficulties to be overcome on these occasions are sometimes very great, and the intense cold makes the operations very trying. A good instance of a successful attack in the face of immense physical difficulties is afforded by the action of the 20th of December, 1891, during the Hunza and Nagar Expedition.

ACTION NEAR NILT FORT,

December 20, 1891.

We have just described* the storming of Nilt Fort on the 2nd December of the same year. Nilt Fort is 6,700 feet above sea level, and stands at the junction of a great ravine with the Hunza River. This ravine has perfectly precipitous sides, varying from 600 feet to 1,500 feet in height, and drains a glacier which lies high up on the Rakapushi Mountain. The Hunza River is a considerable mountain stream and quite unfordable. The enemy held a strong line of sangars along the far side of the ravine, with one flank resting on the river and the other on impassable mountains. For seventeen days the British force lay in Nilt apparently hopelessly checked, though every effort was made, chiefly by means of night reconnaissances, to find some possible line by which this tremendous obstacle could be crossed. At last a bold and enterprising sepoy discovered a way which might be found feasible. Accordingly on the night of the 19th of December one hundred men, under Lieutenants Manners-Smith and Taylor, were ordered to secretly leave Nilt Fort, and under cover of the darkness to drop silently down into the bed of the

* Page 135.

ravine and there await daylight. The portion of the enemy's position which had been selected for attack was towards his extreme left, and fixed on the crest of a precipitous declivity which, without a break, rose 1,500 feet from the bed of the ravine. The remainder of the British force, numbering 135 men, with six British officers and two guns, was detailed to cover the advance of the storming party, by concentrating fire on those of the enemy's defences which lay near the point of attack, thereby not only obliging him to keep under cover, but also preventing him from using the usual deadly tactics of these mountaineers of overwhelming the stormers with an avalanche of rocks. The covering party was entrenched at ranges varying from 400 to 600 yards from the enemy's works.

At 7.55 a.m. fire was opened on the enemy, as it was anticipated that the storming party would be well up the cliff by this time. But unfortunately, after ascending the precipice halfway, Lieutenant Manners-Smith found that he had got on to a part of the cliff which was perfectly impracticable. He had therefore to retrace his steps, every moment adding to the danger of his movements being discovered by the enemy. Descending to the ravine bed he recommenced the ascent at 10 a.m., and this time found a more practicable line. Foot by foot and yard by yard the perilous ascent was made, Lieutenant Manners-Smith manœuvring his small party in the most admirable manner, moving from point to point as opportunity offered between the showers of stones from above. The enemy were now fully aware that the precipice was being scaled, and it was only the well-directed fire of the covering party which prevented their issuing from their bomb-proof defences and annihilating the stormers with rocks and boulders.

At length the summit was reached at 11.30 a.m., and the first of the enemy's works was taken in reverse and captured. Supports were now pushed up, and the whole party of 100 men, under the two British officers, stormed sangar after sangar, by the direction of their attack taking them in flank and rear, and drove the enemy into full flight, killing many and capturing a large number of prisoners. The passage of the great ravine was now gained, and the British force, after nearly three weeks' detention, was enabled to move forward again.

As was noticed in the case of the storming of Nilt Fort, this was another occasion on which great results were obtained, not so much by any great exercise of tactical skill, though the dispositions were indeed all that could be desired, but by the personal leading and influence of the British officers. If Lieutenant Manners-Smith, when he failed in his first attempt to surprise the enemy at dawn, had retired, as he might very well have done, knowing that the undertaking was practically impossible if the enemy found out his exact whereabouts on the cliff, it is quite possible that the passage of the ravine would never have been forced, and the entire expedition thus rendered abortive.

From the foregoing instances it will be gathered that skill, boldness, extreme hardihood, and unflinching self-confidence are necessary to carry an officer successfully through an undertaking of the nature here dealt with. It will be noticed that raids, night surprises, and arduous enterprises of the like description are generally undertaken with detachments composed exclusively of Indian troops, be they Sikhs, Pathans, or Gurkhas, with but a mere sprinkling of British officers. The whole success or failure of the enterprise lies in the leading, and here, without unduly exalting him, it may be said that the British officer excels those of any other nation. He is, as a class, a born leader of men, and more especially so of alien troops, be they Asiatic or African. The presence of but one British officer adds 50 per cent. to the fighting efficiency of a small party, and the splendid feeling of mutual self-confidence which the knowledge of this undoubted fact imparts to all ranks, is responsible for the large majority of brilliant deeds and dashing exploits with which the history of Indian frontier warfare teems.

But whilst living up to the high standard of self-confidence which past exploits give to a British officer, and to the prestige which he possesses, it is possible to strain too highly the actual fighting capabilities of small forces engaged against very superior numbers. Such a case was afforded by the fighting at Chilas.

The post of Chilas had, in March, 1893, been for some time held by 300 men of the Kashmir Maharajah's bodyguard, under the command of two British officers, Major Daniell, of the 1st Punjab Infantry, and Lieutenant Moberly, of the 37th Dogras.

For some time Major Daniell had been in receipt of warnings, which had prepared him for the possibility of being attacked on the night of the Mohamedan feast known as the Shab-i-Barat. Owing to a mistaken calculation, it was understood that the night in question was that of the 3rd March, and when that night had passed quietly it was considered that the storm had blown over. During the night of the 4th, however, a determined attack on the post was made by 1,000 or 1,200 men, and was repulsed by the steady volleys of the garrison.

So far no harm had been suffered from the mistake in dates, but it is open to question whether the further operations would have taken place if fuller information of the enemy's numbers and dispositions had been obtainable, and if the plan of action could have been decided upon after due deliberation, instead of on the spur of the moment, after a severe night attack.

It has elsewhere been mentioned that one of the great endeavours of a British commander in dealing with these ubiquitous mountaineers, is to place them in such a position that they are compelled to fight, being so placed as to make their usual manœuvre of dispersing to collect again on a later occasion impossible. In this endeavour the resources of the British force are occasionally so attenuated as to be weak at all points, running that peculiar danger which threatens an encircling force which pens in, or attempts to pen in, superior numbers, compelled by the nature of their position to fight. The action at Chilas is a ready instance of the dangers incurred in such an undertaking.

It appears that, immediately after the night attack on the fort, Major Daniell determined to take the offensive and to attack the enemy, who had now swarmed into the neighbouring village. Consequently at 3.30 a.m. Lieutenant Moberly, with 35 men, was ordered out to attack the village. After severe fighting and some loss, he effected a lodgment in the outer line of houses, but being shortly after badly wounded, and finding the village too strongly held for his small party to make any further progress, he retired with his detachment to the fort. The enemy kept up a heavy fire on the fort till 8.30 a.m., when it ceased, and Major Daniell determined to issue forth and execute the encircling movement alluded to. The sound of firing and news of the night attack had spread like wildfire amongst the tribes, and it was estimated that there were now from 4,000 to 5,000 armed men collected in the vicinity of Chilas.

Major Daniell for the contemplated enterprise had available only 140 men, the remainder being required to garrison the fort. Issuing therefore from the south-eastern gate of the fort, he made a circuit round the village, and attacked it in two parties, one from the western side and the other from the eastern. He thus encircled the village, having two small parties of seventy men each on two sides, whilst on the third the fort acted as a barrier. After two hours' fighting, during which one of the two attacking parties gained a partial footing in the village, wounded men began to struggle back to the fort, and reported that Major Daniell and many men had been killed and that the attack as a whole had failed. The remnants of the attacking parties were then collected by a native officer and brought safely into the fort at about 11.30 a.m. The casualties in killed and wounded were very heavy, including two British officers, four native officers, and forty-six rank-and-file. The enemy lost about 250 men killed, besides large numbers of wounded. Curiously enough, they did not, however, follow up their success by attacking the fort, and next morning the entire combination, probably thinking that British reinforcements would arrive, had melted away.

In reviewing an action of this description comment is scarcely necessary, but one lesson useful in border warfare may be learnt, and that is that, though great undertakings may be attempted and accomplished with small numbers, yet that there is a point beyond which it is unwise to strain the valour of the troops. They may be highly, very highly, tried, but there is a point beyond which it is not safe to try them. Major Daniell's plan of attack, though extremely gallant, was faulty in conception. To reach the point from which he intended delivering his attack, he had to pass through a raking cross-fire, and the direction of his attack was such as to cause the garrison of the fort to cease fire for fear of hitting his men. He was, it appears, perfectly confident of defeating the enemy, and his only fear was that they would not stand. His attack was, therefore, as we have seen, practically an encircling one, which by cutting off the enemy from all avenues of escape, led to unnecessary loss on our side, while the losses of the enemy were not appreciably increased. If the attack had, on the other hand, been delivered only on the front and flank of the enemy, he would have been driven out into the open ground beyond, suffering severely, whilst our own loss might have been considerably diminished.

It is perhaps hardly necessary to point out that the martial qualities of the tribes and their methods of attack and defence vary very considerably on different parts of the frontier. Whereas in the rocky fastnesses of the north-west the usual defences are stone breastworks (sangars) and stone or mud forts, in the more eastern and densely-wooded parts of the frontier stockades and shelter trenches are the usually defensive works. Each tribe, in fact, uses the materials at hand, and which for generations it has been accustomed to use. It will generally be noticed, too, that the defenders of stockades have not the same grit in fight as their more hardy northern contemporaries, nor are they physically so robust. It is a common thing, therefore, to find stockades, whether held by Thibetans, Burmans, or Shans, boldly rushed by a frontal attack in the many encounters which portions of the Indian Army have had with these people.

Looking to those portions of the frontier which lie to the north-east, we shall find several instructive instances of forest warfare undertaken within recent years. As before mentioned, what is known as the Sikhim Expedition was undertaken in 1888 to re-establish British influence in the territory of that name which lies on the borders of Thibet.

The force employed was as follows:

9—1 Northern Division R.A. (mountain battery), 4 guns.

2nd Battalion Derbyshire Regiment, 200 men.

13th Bengal Infantry, 400 men.

32nd Pioneers, 700 men.

The theatre of operations lay in a very mountainous district, in which the troops had to work at altitudes measuring over 12,000 feet, these mountains being mostly covered with forest trees and dense undergrowth.

The base of operations was at Siliguri, the head of the broad-gauge railway, and the advance base at Padong, thirty miles north-east of Darjeeling. A distance of forty miles only separated the advance from the first objective of the expedition, which was the fort of Lingtu. Working at this high altitude and through country affording the immense physical difficulties which had to be encountered, only men reported in every way fit for an arduous campaign in a cold climate were allowed to accompany the force.

Ammunition calculated at the rate of 168 rounds per gun, 200 rounds per rifle, and 100 rounds per carbine was carried.

Tents were allowed on the usual scale, a tent weighing 160 pounds being apportioned to sixteen men.

In addition to the usual entrenching tools, 100 daos or native short swords were issued to each regiment, and 50 to each battery, whilst fifty per cent. of the followers were similarly supplied. These daos were used for clearing away jungle and cutting firewood.

Supplies were collected for one month, and the transport consisted of mules, supplemented by coolies. The extension of the telegraph line and the postal arrangements were carried out by the civil departments.

The force was concentrated at Padong and ready to start by the middle of March, and the 16th of that month was selected for the advance. The column was divided into two detachments, the first consisting of two mountain guns, 100 men of the Derbyshire Regiment, and 300 men of the 32nd Pioneers, under Colonel Graham, R.A., proceeding direct towards Lingtu, whilst the second, under Colonel Mitchell, consisting of two mountain guns, 100 men of the Derbyshire Regiment, and 300 men of the 13th Bengal Infantry, was directed to proceed towards Intchi, where the Sikhim Raja was then residing. The operations of these two columns were practically distinct, not being within lateral communication of each other, and having divergent objectives. The latter column met with no opposition, and after demonstrating towards Intchi was withdrawn.

The first column, after marching on the 17th, 18th, and 19th, came across the enemy at Jeluk, about five miles short of Lingtu. A reconnaissance showed that the Thibetans had erected a stockade on the top of a very steep ascent, and had barricaded the road with a stone breastwork. Colonel Graham commenced his advance on this position at 7 a.m. The attacking party consisted of 100 men of the 32nd Pioneers, supported by 78 men of the Derbyshire Regiment. The guns, though carried on mules, had to be left behind, owing to the badness of the track. The advance could only be made with great deliberation, as, owing to the dense bamboo jungle through which the road passed, and also the steepness of the road itself and its many windings, great caution was necessary. On reaching a spot within a few hundred yards of the stockade fire was suddenly opened on the Pioneers. But these fine troops moved steadily on without replying, till, having worked their way close up to the stockade, they fired a volley, and then with a loud cheer boldly charged with the bayonet straight at the centre of the stockade, their Colonel, Sir Benjamin Bromhead, being the first into the work. The Derbyshire detachment moving up in support, the main position was captured after a short struggle, and the enemy pursued along the Lingtu road. To aid this frontal attack Sir Benjamin Bromhead had, when he commenced his final advance, detached a turning party to his left under Captain H. R. W. Lumsden; but this party, after proceeding a short distance, found the path cut clean away at a point where it passed round a precipice, and defended by a party of the enemy in a stone breastwork at ten yards range. Captain Lumsden and several of his men were knocked over, and the turning party was completely baffled. So thick was the jungle that neither side could know what was going on at the main stockade, and the first intimation that arrived of the success of the frontal attack was by the descent of a party of the Derbyshire Regiment on the rear of the party of the enemy in the stone breastwork.

When the main position came to be examined it was found to be a most formidable one. The stockade was about 200 yards long, running along the crest of the ridge, both flanks resting on impassable precipices. It was constructed of large logs laid horizontally, whilst trees felled in front formed a thick abattis. The only approach was a purely frontal one, up a precipitous ascent. The garrison consisted of 120 men, some of the marksmen being posted in trees.

It will be noticed that the number of defenders was insufficient for the size of the work. Three hundred determined men, well armed, could hold such a position against an army.

Next morning the advance on Lingtu was continued in a dense mist. A Thibetan prisoner gave the useful information that a stone-shoot, by means of which an avalanche of rocks and stones could be hurled on the attackers, had to be crossed before reaching the vicinity of the fort. The force, therefore, advanced with the utmost caution, leaving 350 yards interval between each unit, whilst a party of the Pioneers crept along the crest of the ridge to take in rear the party manning the stone-shoot.

The mist was so dense that it was impossible to see more than fifty yards in any direction; the road was steep and broken, and the partially melted snow gradually increased in depth till it lay two feet deep on the road. Feeling his way with the greatest caution, Colonel Bromhead succeeded in capturing the stone-shoot and crossing it without loss. He then pushed straight up the precipitous hill, and without firing a shot charged straight at the fort, and had burst his way through the main gate before the astonished Thibetans could open fire. The defenders immediately fled and were pursued by the Pioneers.

The Fort (so called) of Lingtu was constructed on the same principle as the defences at Jeluk, but with this important difference, that its flanks did not rest on impassable obstacles, but merely consisted of stone towers. A straight wall, whether resting on two towers or not, is naturally as feeble a description of work as can be constructed, and the Lingtu structure may perhaps be looked upon chiefly as a work of bravado, being built, as it was, right across and barring a trade route previously constructed by the British. The object of the expedition had now been accomplished, the Thibetans expelled from Sikhim territory, and the road re-opened.

Against an enemy of such poor fighting calibre as the Thibetans the difficulties of a campaign do not rest so much in the resistance of the enemy as in negotiating the physical and climatic difficulties which the country affords. Dense jungle, deep snow, mist and rain, with roads almost impassable, winding up precipitous mountains, all afford problems which try very highly the resources of a commander. Administrative skill, combined with great dash and boldness, rather than tactical or strategical skill, would seem to be required in warfare of this description. At the same time it must be remembered that rashness which led even to a temporary check might seriously jeopardise the safety of the whole force. Campaigning in semi-barbarous regions such as these may be likened to skating on very thin ice—a bold dash is successful, but wavering begets disaster.

Though there is scope for little tactics and less strategy, in the common acceptance of those terms, in an operation of this description, yet it brings forward one more instance of what bold leading and a determined assault can do even under the most unfavourable circumstances. In common military parlance, Jeluk was an impregnable position, to attack which by the only way open was to undertake a purely frontal and consequently costly attack. Yet, with the loss of five wounded, the stockade was taken.

Another instance of attack on a stockade may be quoted from the Burmah War. A column consisting of 190 men, made up of 100 men of "The Queen's," 30 men of the Somersetshire Light Infantry, 30 men of the 3rd Madras Light Infantry, and 30 men of the 1st Beluch Light Infantry, under Colonel Holt, of "The Queen's," marched from Pyinmana on the 30th of November to dislodge the rebel leader, Sam Pé, from his position at Saikpuduang. Owing to scarcity of carriage, only four days' rations could be taken with the column. The rebels were found in a strong position, with the approaches spiked.* The position consisted of a formidable stockade, flanked on each side by precipitous hills, which were held in force. The advance guard, though moving with great caution, at a bend in the path came suddenly full on to the front of a breast-

* Covered with bamboo spikes known as panjies.—ED.

work, from which a heavy fire was immediately poured into them, wounding two or three men. Colonel Holt thereupon ordered a party under Captain Boddam to work round to the left, and to turn the enemy's flank. As soon as the effect of the flank movement began to tell, a frontal attack with the bayonet was ordered, and the stockade was assaulted and captured with a loss of six men.

This is one of the many instances where, in spite of every caution, the nature of the country made it impossible to exactly locate the enemy's position till it was actually confronted at a range of only a few paces. The decisive effect of a flank movement, even though the flanking party consists of but a few men, is here clearly demonstrated. On this occasion, unlike the generality of cases, the enemy had made some attempt to secure his flanks by holding the two precipitous hills on either side, but his rear was apparently quite unprotected, either by troops or stockades. Indeed, the Burman's idea of defence is typified by his expression of astonishment on finding that the British, in making stockades, or fortified posts, arranged for an all-round defence. "But which side do you run away from?" he asks. The reason of which question is to be found in the fact that a Burmese stockade usually has three defensive sides, the fourth side being left open, so that no obstacle to a speedy retreat may be encountered.

CHAPTER VI.

CONVOYS.

Not the least important duty which falls on troops engaged in frontier warfare is the work of protecting convoys. As has been mentioned in other chapters, those frontier districts which are usually the theatre of war are practically devoid of supplies, in so far even as a force of a few thousand men is concerned. A hundred men here and there can, no doubt, be supported for a few days or a few weeks by the country, but any operations that are necessarily prolonged, and in which a force of any strength takes part, involve a constant flow of provisions from the base in rear. These supplies are pushed to the front on pack animals, or, where the roads allow of it, on carts. Such trains are on most parts of the frontier in constant danger throughout each march as they move up from stage to stage, and are not infrequently in need of protection for every mile of the road.

A convoy of only two or three hundred animals, generally moving in single file, covers a considerable amount of road, and the problem is, how most safely to guard them without unduly harassing the troops.

The two systems in vogue are: (1) Armed escorts which march with the convoy, and (2) a chain of daily piquets which hold important points on the route.

It depends chiefly on the nature of the country to decide which form of protection is the most suitable.

In cramped mountainous districts, where the road runs through defiles or along narrow valleys, and where it is commanded on all sides, it will generally be found that a chain of piquets, placed at advantageous points, will serve the purpose best. On the other hand, in level country, whether open or forest-covered, it is generally considered more suitable to have a moving escort distributed in convenient-sized parties along the line of the convoy. Thus, on the road from Peshawur to Kabul, during the 1878-80 campaign, those portions which ran through the Khyber and Jugdulluk passes were guarded by infantry day piquets, sent out every morning halfway on both sides from each permanent post, a small cavalry escort, more for police duties than as a protection, accompanying the convoy; whilst in the open valleys of Jellalabad and Kabul mixed cavalry and infantry escorts, relieved halfway, accompanied the convoys throughout, and no piquets were considered necessary. Though it is rarely possible in frontier expeditions to dispense entirely with escorts and convoys, it is not necessary to go to the other extreme and to harass the troops unnecessarily by employing large bodies of men for their protection. Systematic warfare is practically unknown amongst the border tribes, and such attacks as are made on convoys are more generally the work of prowling bands of marauders or fanatics, rather than the result of a carefully devised method of crippling their enemy's resources. Even when these attacks are pushed home and are apparently most successful, it eventually proves that the harm done in most cases has been infinitesimal—at the most, perhaps, resulting in the loss of a bag or two of grain and half a dozen animals seized, a native driver or two being wounded perhaps in the struggle.

The confusion that occurs in a convoy when it is attacked, especially if it be in thick bush, is naturally great, and to those on the spot it appears for the moment as if matters were in a desperate state. But as a rule the effect is merely local and temporary. The road on which the convoy is moving is very generally the only one; a strong force of troops or a fortified post lies at each end of the march, and the escort to the convoy, or the nearest piquet, cannot be far off. Therefore, there is little or no chance, with ordinary precaution, for even the most enterprising enemy to capture or carry off the convoy as a whole or even any considerable portion of it.

An exception to this general rule was afforded by the complete capture of a convoy by the enemy during the advance on Kabul in 1880. The loss was directly due to disobedience of orders, the convoy having started without the knowledge of Brigadier-General Baker, and being accompanied by a much smaller escort than the minimum ordered. The convoy consisted of one telegraph linesman, twenty-two telegraph coolies, forty muleteers, and eighty-four unloaded mules, proceeding for the purpose of bringing up telegraph poles from Karatiga to the Shutargurdan Pass. The escort was composed of one naik and ten sepoys of the 5th Punjab Infantry. The Brigadier's order being that escorts were to be calculated out on the scale of one soldier to every four mules or other pack animals, it will be noticed that the escort was less than half the strength ordered.

The convoy started for Karatiga at 6 a.m., and at 9 a.m. intelligence reached the Shutargurdan that not only had this party been attacked, but also that a heavy fire had been kept up upon the detachment, consisting of one British officer and fifty non-commissioned officers and men stationed in a blockhouse on the Surkhi Kotal, which lay not far from the point of attack. As many of the 72nd Highlanders as could be spared were at once despatched to the spot where the convoy had been attacked, but arrived too late to be of any assistance, the marauders having disappeared, and all attempts to follow them up proved useless. The attacking party consisted of Mangal and Ghilzai mountaineers and numbered from 200 to 300 men. The escort of the 5th Punjab Infantry fought against these tremendous odds with the greatest gallantry, the non-commissioned officer and six of his ten men being killed and one wounded in the fight. Of the convoy, one telegraph linesman, twelve muleteers, and six telegraph coolies were killed, and two muleteers wounded; whilst the enemy captured all the mules, numbering eighty-four, and one muleteer and two coolies were impressed to help drive them off.

It will be noticed that the attack was made with some science and skill. The road had probably been watched for days, the spot carefully chosen, and a simultaneous attack was made on the blockhouse at Surki Kotal, so as to prevent any assistance reaching the convoy. But such carefully-made attacks are rare, the semi-barbarous tradition still lingering with these wild men, as with the Chinese, that to make a great deal of noise, hurl virulent abuse, brandish swords and fire off guns, produces a moral effect which must eventually lead to success.

Therefore, although such attacks on convoys as occur are annoying, they cannot be considered in any sensible degree to affect the even flow of the operations.

By an intelligent use of spies, renegades, and the hundred and one men who are to be bought with a few rupees, it should be possible always to have timely notice of the presence of marauding bands who may happen to collect anywhere within striking distance of the road which the convoys follow, and, taking the initiative, to deal with these, with troops unconnected with the escort of the convoy, before it reaches the threatened points. No greater security can be afforded than by assuming a strong and active offensive of this nature.

It is a generally accepted rule in civilized warfare that in attacking a convoy the attack should be concentrated on the escort, because, when this is disposed of, the convoy falls an easy prey to the attackers. This principle is, however, very rarely acted upon by the border tribes. On the other hand, their attacking parties will usually carefully avoid the escort, and will attack that portion of a convoy which is apparently the weakest. So much annoyance, though loss there was none to speak of, was caused by attacks of this description on convoys of carts moving through the Khyber Pass during the winter of 1878-79, that it was decided to ambuscade the ambuscaders. To effect this, at the weakest portion of a long line of carts, purposely left to all appearance quite unprotected, one or two carts, instead of being filled with bags of grain, were filled with armed men, carefully covered over and concealed from view. The moral effect of this device was much on a par with that which results from the springing of a mine on an enemy. The actual loss may be infinitesimal, but the moral advantage gained is often very great. Thus, in this case, the enemy having once, to use a familiar term, "caught a Tartar," found that the pastime of attacking convoys began to lose its charm, and more especially were seemingly unguarded lines of carts avoided.

Another form of ambuscade, which was found effective in Burmah, was exemplified during the march of the Mainlung column on January 28th, 1887. During the day before, owing chiefly to the carelessness of the drivers, a party of Shans captured some thirty or forty baggage ponies. A party under Lieutenant Brocklehurst recaptured all but sixteen of these, but on the following morning information was received that the Shans were contemplating following the baggage in the hope of further captures. Colonel Deshon, who was commanding, therefore ordered the rearguard of twenty-five men of the Somersetshire Light Infantry, under Lieutenant Morse, after marching off the ground as usual, to form an ambuscade. Lieutenant Morse had hardly got into the jungle when the Shans were on him; he killed four and the remainder fled. Continuing his march, he repeated the same manœuvre, concealing himself under cover of a convenient spur. The Shans, who were creeping after him, were again surprised and completely routed. After this they troubled the rearguard no more.

It is a recognized principle with long convoys, moving on single-file roads, when attacked, that the drivers should not halt, but should keep pushing on, leaving the escort to deal with the enemy. Thus, during the Burmah War, whilst a detachment of the 3rd Madras Infantry, consisting of 100 rifles under Lieutenant-Colonel Anderson, was marching from Gwebin to Pyokgôn in charge of a large convoy of 77 carts, they were suddenly attacked by a considerable force of dacoits near Kanhla. The jungle was so dense that no enemy could be seen at even a few paces distant, and the view to front and rear was restricted by the tortuous nature of the road. At the moment that the attack was made the escort was disposed as follows:

> Twenty rifles advance guard; fifty rifles divided into parties of five each, and distributed along the line of carts; and twenty rifles as a rearguard.

When the convoy had reached a point a short distance south of Kanhla, a volley was fired into the advance party of the advance guard, which consisted of two non-commissioned officers and three men. The volley was fired pointblank, at twenty yards range, with Snider rifles, and four out of five composing the advance party were killed on the spot. Colonel Anderson immediately pushed on with the main body of the advance guard, and was severely wounded. His men kept on advancing, firing volleys more or less at haphazard into the bush to front and flanks, for no enemy was visible. The fire, however, was evidently effective, for the enemy evacuated the prepared position which barred the road. This consisted of a breastwork of felled trees, and so hurried was their flight that 100 Snider cartridges were left on the ground. Meanwhile the rearguard, consisting of twenty men, was charged by thirty or forty men armed with daos, many of whom were killed by the volleys which greeted their attack. After two hours' fighting, during which time the convoy was kept moving, the enemy was beaten off.

On the 18th April, 1886, during the Burmah War, a party consisting of twenty rifles under a jemadar started from Hlaingdet to Meiktila in charge of a convoy of provisions. After proceeding nine miles, the convoy was suddenly attacked at a place called Menhla, and three men were wounded. But the convoy pushed steadily on as far as Kong-Daung, where it halted for the night. During the evening the convoy, which was now concentrated, was surrounded and attacked on all sides by from 2,000 to 3,000 of the enemy, a heavy fire being kept up all night, whereby four more of the escort were wounded. There were now only thirteen men fit for duty. News had, however, reached Hlaingdet the evening before of the hazardous position of the convoy, and Lieutenant

Forbes was at once despatched with twenty rifles of the Liverpool Regiment and thirty rifles of the 11th Bengal Infantry to its assistance. Making an all-night march, Lieutenant Forbes came up with the convoy in the early morning, and joining with the jemadar's party, drove off the enemy. He then put the convoy in motion and reached his destination, Meiktila, without further fighting.

A return convoy had now to start back from Meiktila to Hlaingdet, and Lieutenant Forbes, in command of a party of seventy men, was detailed as escort. He started on the morning of the 20th, and marched all day. When night fell he massed his convoy on an open piece of ground clear of jungle, and took up a position to protect it. All night the party was fired upon by the enemy, who, however, kept at a distance and did not attempt to rush the bivouac. No loss occurred during the night. On the morning of the 21st the convoy again started, and when about six miles from Hlaingdet came across a large body of the enemy blocking the road and lining the jungle on both sides. The escort was formed with the twenty men of the Liverpool Regiment as a first line in skirmishing order, whilst Lieutenant Forbes, with twenty sepoys, formed the support, and thirty sepoys were with the convoy in rear. During the advance, Lieutenant Forbes was shot through the heart, but the escort fought its way through the jungle and reached Hlaingdet in safety with the convoy complete. The enemy lost in killed alone 123 men.

It might at first appear that to start a convoy with an escort of only twenty men, to make a two days' march in the face of 2,000 to 3,000 of the enemy, would be to court the loss of the entire convoy. Undoubtedly in this case the escort was too weak, but when the convoy started such reliable information as could be obtained pointed only to the presence of small bands of dacoits, with whom a few determined men could deal successfully. As soon as the escort was augmented to seventy men under a British officer it will be noticed that the convoy pushed steadily through, both on the outward and return journeys, and that it reached its journey's end on each occasion without any loss in stores or animals.

In marked contrast to the general rule, the protection of convoys during the operations for the relief of Chitral proved to be devoid of trouble or risk. So sharp, unexpected and effective were the blows dealt by the relieving force that the whole country remained as if paralysed. And though it was necessary to hold for five months a line of communications 200 miles in length, convoys could move practically without protection, and not a single case of attack occurred.

Occasionally a large force has to make a prolonged march, carrying the whole or part of its supplies and baggage with it. Instances in point are the march of Sir Donald Stewart's force to Kabul and Sir Frederick Roberts' march from Kabul to Kandahar for the relief of that place. During such marches the whole force is practically an escort to the convoy, and its preservation is a matter of vital importance.

Sir Donald Stewart's force consisted of three brigades, and he had, besides tents and baggage, to carry with him such supplies for the Europeans as were unobtainable in the country through which his division would have to pass. From Kandahar up to Mukur, a distance of 155 miles, the brigades were able to march independently, each convoying its own supplies and baggage. But from Mukur onwards, towards Ghazni, owing to the proximity of the enemy, the division had to march in a more concentrated formation, and on the morning of the battle of Ahmed Kheyl we find it marching thus: Advance guard—

19th Bengal Lancers.
A. Battery, B. Brigade R.H.
19th Punjab Infantry.
Nos. 4 and 10 Companies Bengal Sappers and Miners.

The Divisional Headquarters, with its escort of one company 60th Rifles, one company 25th Punjab Infantry, and half a squadron of the 19th Bengal Lancers, accompanied the advance guard.

Next came the main body, consisting of the 2nd Brigade, numbering 1,092 rifles, 349 sabres, and ten guns. Behind this brigade were the whole of the baggage and supply trains, with detachments of troops on the flanks.

In rear of the baggage and supply trains came the 1st Brigade, numbering 1,393 rifles, 316 sabres, and six mountain guns.

The force was in fact disposed as a large convoy for the protection of its own supplies. As will be noticed in the account of the battle previously given,* the

* Page 100.

attack came neither on the front nor on the rear, both of which were very strongly guarded, but on the flank. Directly he was threatened, Sir Donald Stewart, knowing the efficacy of taking the initiative, formed front to a flank and was preparing to deliver an attack with his leading brigade as the best method of clearing the road, when the enemy suddenly burst upon him and compelled him to take up a defensive attitude. The attack of the enemy, though most bold and spirited, was in this case undoubtedly misdirected. For though as a rule it is a sound principle to first attack the escort, yet there are occasions when, as in the present case, the vital point lies elsewhere. The line of baggage and supplies was six miles long, and its chief strength lay in its head and rear, each consisting of a brigade. If the enemy, therefore, had allowed the leading brigade to commit itself to the attack that was contemplated, leaving merely a skeleton force before it to entice it on, and then, with his main force of many thousand irregular cavalry and infantry, seizing a favourable moment, had swept down on the baggage and supplies, the blow might have been a most effective one. For it must be remembered that the British division was practically *en l'air*, and was very largely, if not entirely, dependent on the stores which it carried with it. The partial or complete loss of these stores would undoubtedly have placed it in the most hazardous position.

The march of Sir Frederick Roberts from Kabul to Kandahar furnishes another instance of a convoy on a large scale; and though he was not attacked *en route*, the arrangements made for the protection of his supplies and baggage are very instructive.

THE MARCH FROM KABUL TO KANDAHAR.

It will be remembered that a British force was defeated at Maiwand on July 27th, 1880, by an Afghan force under Ayoub Khan which was advancing from Herat on Kandahar. As a result of the defeat, General Primrose's division was shut up in Kandahar and closely besieged. To relieve it a force of 10,000 men under Sir Frederick Roberts was despatched from Kabul on August 8th. From Kabul to Kandahar is just over 300 miles, and no made roads connected the two places. The route lay through a hostile country, and the force, during its march, would be cut off from all communication with its base, or with India. As Colonel E. F. Chapman, who accompanied the force, writes: "A march conducted without a base of operations or communications of any kind, through a hostile country, and towards a point presumably in the possession of an enemy who had recently been successful, could only be warranted by such necessity as had now arisen; in this instance, however, the wisdom that prompted the measure and the courage which executed it sprang of experience and of the confidence which claims success as a certainty. The result justified the conception, and the march from Kabul to Kandahar has been recognized as a great achievement. It will be remembered that at the time it was undertaken and until a crushing defeat had been inflicted on Ayoub Khan at Kandahar itself, the movement was condemned, in no measured terms, by military critics, its originators being judged to have acted in complete disregard of the principles of military science. With troops, however, trained and equipped as were those selected for the undertaking, a commander may, humanly speaking, anticipate success in any enterprise." The arrangements made at Kabul for the despatch of the force were the result of the experience gained during nearly two years of continuous field service, and the men were veterans all, inured to fatigue and of the highest fighting quality, whilst their equipment was in first-class order.

The force consisted of three brigades of infantry, each brigade being composed of two British and two native regiments; a cavalry brigade, consisting of one British and three native cavalry regiments; three mule batteries of mountain artillery; the engineer park, ordnance park, hospital, commissariat, etc.—making a total of 9,987 fighting men and 18 guns.

The transport train consisted of 1,589 ponies, 4,511 mules, 1,149 small ponies, and 912 donkeys. The number of native camp-followers was about 7,000.

The force marched from Kabul on the 8th August, making as its first objective the fortress of Ghazni, distant 89 miles. This point was reached on the seventh day, after some arduous marching, including a march of 18 miles across the Zamburak Kotal, 8,100 feet above the sea. During some of the marches the rearguard did not arrive in camp till nightfall, though the column started at 4 a.m.

The order of march issued on August 10th directed the cavalry brigade to move well in front, and laid down that, when two or more infantry brigades were marching together, the following would be the order of march:

(1) Troops constituting the fighting line, with the first reserve of ammunition, rations and cooking pots for British regiments, dhoolies and dandies.

(2) Field hospitals, ordnance park, treasure, engineer park, led horses. The baggage of brigades massed, and moving in order of march of their corps.

(3) The rearguard (as may be detailed).

The brigades generally managed to find parallel routes by which to march, but were often restricted to one road during the passage of defiles, etc.

Fifteen miles short of Ghazni the force was united, as it was uncertain whether fighting would be necessary, and a detachment was sent on to seize the Sher-Dáhar Pass. Ghazni was, however, occupied without resistance, the governor coming out to meet the troops and presenting the keys of the fortress to the general.

The next phase of the march was from Ghazni to Khelat-i-Ghilzai, a distance of 136 miles, or a total distance from Kabul of 225 miles. This point was reached on the eighth day from Ghazni, and the 15th day from Kabul. The march as far as Khelat-i-Ghilzai had been made without a day's halt. For the first three marches out of Ghazni all the brigades had to use one road, which severely tried the endurance of both men and baggage animals. Water, too, was often scarce, and the first march from Ghazni had to be extended to 20 miles to reach a very indifferent supply. On the 11th day the force came to sufficiently open country to allow of the brigades moving on roads parallel to each other. The centre brigade was nominated the brigade of direction and each brigade was followed by its own baggage, that of the cavalry moving behind the baggage of the centre brigade. Rearguards were formed of two companies from each of the four regiments of each brigade. Each brigade, therefore, had a rearguard of the strength of one regiment.

The reason for not detailing a complete unit, such as a battalion, as rearguard for each brigade, or a complete brigade as rearguard for the whole division, was twofold. In the first place no danger was to be anticipated from the rear, any concentrated force of the enemy being well away to the front; therefore there was no tactical reason against having the rearguard composed of small units from different corps. On the other hand, the practical advantage was great. For in all operations where pack animals are used the careful loading of the animals is of the greatest importance and requires considerable skill and practice. Careless loading means constant and serious delay to the rearguard. If a soldier, or company of soldiers, or a battalion, finds that careless loading recoils on their own heads, in that they spend the whole march in picking up and reloading baggage and supplies, the evil is very soon rectified. It was found expedient, therefore, in the long and trying marches that Sir Frederick Roberts' force had to make, that each battalion should furnish its fair proportion of the rearguard. Each regiment and each brigade thus became responsible for its own goods, and common interest thus prevented a loss in stores which, as the animals became weaker, would under any other system have been very great.

At Khelat-i-Ghilzai was found a British garrison which had been detached from Kandahar before these troubles began. News by heliograph had been received of the disastrous sortie from Kandahar, made on August 16th, in which the casualties were Brigadier General Brook, and fifteen officers and 175 men killed or wounded.

A halt of one day was made at Khelat-i-Ghilzai to give the force a much-earned rest. The third phase of the march was from Khelat-i-Ghilzai to Kandahar, a distance of 76 miles, or a total distance from Kabul of 301 miles. This last stage was covered in six marches.

The country passed through was not difficult, though generally sufficiently enclosed to prevent an advance being made on a broad front.

At Rabat, 20 miles short of Kandahar, Sir Frederick Roberts got into direct communication by heliograph with Kandahar, and was later met by two British officers who had been sent out to meet him.

On August 31st, the force reached Kandahar.

Sir Frederick Roberts immediately reconnoitred the enemy's position, and on the next day, September 1st, attacked and defeated Ayoub Khan with great slaughter, capturing the whole of his artillery, his stores, and his camp as it stood.

The march had occupied twenty-one marching days and there were two days' halt, one at Khelat-i-Ghilzai and the other at Rabat. The average rate of marching throughout had, therefore, been just under an average of 14½ miles a day, exclusive of halts. This, it must be remembered, during one of the hottest months in the year.

The force arrived with 940 sick, mostly slight cases of sore feet. Three men died during the march, and a few stragglers were cut off by the enemy. The condition of the cavalry horses and of the transport animals is reported as very good, and the splendid appearance of the troops as they marched in after their arduous undertaking was the admiration of all.

From these examples a fairly correct idea may be gained of the methods employed for the protection of convoys, both small and great, in dealing with such enemies as are met under the different local conditions on our Indian Frontiers.

CHAPTER VII.

Mountain Artillery.

It is rarely possible to use horse or field artillery, owing to the difficulty of the country and the absence of roads in purely border warfare. When, however, we issue into the valleys and plains of Afghanistan, wheeled artillery takes its place with the other arms. The action of wheeled artillery is, however, on purely European lines, and therefore it will not be necessary to enlarge here on a subject which is fully dealt with in the authorized Drill Book. But there is in India a special branch of the regiment called Mountain Artillery, and which can alone be made available in mountain warfare. The principle acted upon is to substitute pack mules for carriages; and with due regard to the carrying capacity of a mule to have the most powerful and most suitable gun procurable.

In the early days of rifled Mountain Artillery the ordnance in use was a 7-pr. gun, made in one piece, and weighing about 200 lbs. This gun partook somewhat of the nature of a howitzer, suitable for pitching shells into forts and searching the reverse slopes of an enemy's position. But it was defective in range and not very accurate as to direction. To improve the gun by lengthening it and increasing its calibre, whilst it remained in one piece, was impossible, owing to the limited carrying capacity of a pack animal; but the invention of jointed guns solved the difficulty.

The gun now in use is made in two pieces, each

carried on a separate mule, which, before the gun comes into action, are screwed together.

Each battery consists of six guns, with a complement of 138 ordnance mules, which are thus apportioned:

	Right subdivisions of sections.		*Left subdivisions.*
Chase, breech, axle, wheels, carriage	5		5
Relief	5		5
Ammunition	6		6
Relief ammunition	1		1
Pioneer	1		
		Artificers' boxes	1
		Spare wheels	1
		Relief wheels	1
Bare backs	4		4
	22		24

Total in battery:—138 ordnance mules,
76 transport mules,
6 ponies.

The loads carried by the different mules are as follows:

	lbs.	oz.
Chase	285	5
Breech	293	10
Wheels	280	10
Axle	267	6
Carriage	295	
Ammunition	367	10¾
Pioneer equipment	324	6¾

In addition to the wheels, the "wheel mule" carries the elevating gear.

The total amount of ammunition carried by a battery is 216 ring-shell, 540 shrapnel, 108 case, 12 star.

The average height of the mules is 13-3 hands, which is found the best working height. Larger mules are difficult to load and unload, whilst smaller ones are not up to the weights to be carried.

A battery takes one minute and ten seconds to get into action, and about the same time to dismount the guns and move off again. There are eight British Mountain Batteries and eight Native Mountain Batteries, the latter being officered by British officers. The eight British Mountain Batteries are armed with the 2′ 5″ R.M.L. screw-gun, and the Native Mountain Batteries partially with the same gun and partially with the 7-pr. R.M.L. gun, weighing 200 pounds. The intention is to have all batteries with the same armament, and this will be effected when artillery experts have finally decided on the best gun for the purpose.

The mule is not only a very hardy animal, but very sure-footed, and it may be broadly stated that, wherever infantry can go in the mountains, mountain artillery can manage to get within effective range of its opponents.

The tactics of mountain artillery are the same as those of other branches of the artillery arm. They consist of an endeavour to so place the guns as best to assist the infantry attack or infantry defence, as the case may be, and to concentrate their fire.*

In fighting against the border tribes, who are themselves either devoid of artillery, or, at best, possessed of a few obsolete smooth-bores, the moral effect of guns is naturally very considerable, and this moral effect is much enhanced by the ubiquitous nature of the mountain gun, and the excellent shooting it makes.

It would appear at first that a battery carried on mules was a very vulnerable arm, and liable both on the march and in action to be seriously incapacitated by the loss of the mules. This danger has certainly to be faced, and in fighting against European troops the greatest precautions would be necessary to avoid undue loss. It will be noticed that each mule which carries a part of a gun or its carriage, has a relief mule available for replacing casualties in action as well as for taking its share of the work on the march.

In the few cases where it has been necessary to resort to coolie carriage for the guns, the results have not been satisfactory.† To transport guns by this method during a prolonged campaign is practically impossible, for not only is the feed of the coolies a very serious item, but they appear to be unable to stand the prolonged strain, and as likely as not their hearts fail them when they come under fire; with the result that the guns may be left stranded on the very

* The advantages of concentrating artillery fire are plainly shown in the recent advance of Sir W. Lockhart's force into the Afridi country, November, 1897.—ED.

† On the West Coast of Africa, however, coolies have been used for this purpose with success.—ED.

verge of the field of battle. Where mules cannot go, therefore, it will be found wiser for a commander not, as a rule, to attempt to take guns.

There are occasions, however, and places, where elephants can be called into requisition in place of mules. Thus where many deep streams have to be crossed, thick low undergrowth to be pushed through, and even in moderately swampy ground an elephant will move steadily forward unhampered, where a heavily loaded mule would barely struggle along. In Afghanistan, Horse Artillery guns were, when there was a lack of Mountain Artillery, placed on elephants for carriage through regions impassable for wheels, with satisfactory results.

Rarely a year passes without one or other of the mountain batteries seeing service, and in some years all are employed on different parts of the frontier. The experience thus gained in practical mountain warfare has raised this service to the highest pitch of excellence, and throughout the Army in India there is no more thoroughly and practically efficient arm than the Mountain Artillery.

CHAPTER VIII.

Cavalry and Mounted Infantry.

As will have been gathered from previous chapters, the frontiers of India, consisting as they do for the most part of mountain chains, or great forest-covered hills and plains, do not lend themselves to the action of cavalry manœuvred in large bodies. At the best, difficult passes give access to restricted valleys; narrow and stone-strewn defiles lead to equally inhospitable regions, and single-file tracks running through dense forest culminate only in small village clearings. In such regions the *rôle* of cavalry is naturally much restricted, and the effective action of any body greater than a squadron is rarely possible. On one face only, when once we pass through the mountain barrier, do we come to country favourable for the use of larger bodies. This is on the western frontier, where the borders of Afghanistan and Beluchistan march contiguous with our own. Nor need we forget, though the subject does not come into the scope of this book, that in the event of internal trouble in India, the use of cavalry on a large scale would naturally form a most important part in all operations.

As the organization of the Indian cavalry is on somewhat a different basis to that usually obtaining in other armies, it may not be inappropriate, before entering into the work, past and to come, of this branch of the Indian Army, to describe in some detail the system on which it is raised and maintained.

The cavalry service, like the rest of the Indian Army, is purely voluntary. In some measures also it is almost feudatory, for every recruit who joins the service brings voluntarily with him a horse and all its accoutrements, and his uniform, arms, and equipment, or as an alternative the equivalent thereof in money. The only portion of his outfit which is supplied by Government is a carbine. It is more economical for a man to bring money. He has, therefore, in latter days, almost invariably done so. The actual sum which a recruit is expected to bring with him, on enlistment, in lieu of horse and equipment, varies in different regiments, the matter being left in the hands of the commanding officer. Generally speaking, the sum varies from Rs. 250 to Rs. 400. In special cases, however, good fighting men are taken at a lower figure, but deductions are made from their pay till the full sum is made good. The total sum thus raised forms the working capital of the regiment.

A regiment, or rather the individuals that compose it, are, as regards their masters, the Government of India, on a purely contract system. The Government hands over so many rupees *per mensem* to each British officer, native officer, or man; and in return expects each to be in every way, and at all points, ready to take the field at the shortest notice. The sum paid by Government to each man in the ranks, who places himself under this obligation, is Rs. 31* monthly. This, at present rates, is about equivalent to thirty-five

* Increased after stated periods by the addition of "good conduct" pay.

shillings. For thirty-five shillings a month an Indian cavalry trooper feeds and keeps himself and his horse; renews his uniform; pays for half a share in the purchase and feed and keep of a baggage pony; pays half the wages of one syce; builds and keeps up his horse and pony standings, and his own hut; pays his share towards keeping up all necessary artificers and servants, such as sword sharpeners, cooks, sweepers, etc.; in fact, in return for his pay he is entirely self-supporting. Probably this is the cheapest cavalry service that exists, more especially so taking into consideration the high state of efficiency which it has reached.

It may perhaps be wondered how recruits can be found who will enlist on such seemingly disadvantageous terms. But living, as far as the native ranks are concerned, is cheap in India, for a man need not spend more than Rs. 6 on his food during the month. The feed of his horse will cost on an average from Rs. 4 to Rs. 5. The cost of his half share in a syce* and half share in the feed of a baggage pony comes to about Rs. 4 a month. Subscriptions and renewals to uniform and saddlery mount up to, say Rs. 5 or Rs. 6. The total output is, therefore, about Rs. 20; so that the trooper receives clear, in good times, ten or eleven rupees a month in return for his services. According to European rates this would appear to be poor remuneration, but it is good pay in India, and attracts all the best fighting classes into our ranks.

* The syce, in return for his pay, not only helps to groom the horse, but provides its grass.

Each regiment consists of four squadrons, each squadron having an approximate strength of 150 of all ranks. All regiments are permanently maintained at full war strength in men, horses, and baggage animals. There are nineteen regiments of Bengal cavalry, four regiments of Punjab cavalry, seven regiments of Bombay cavalry, three regiments of Madras cavalry, two regiments of Central India Horse, four regiments of Hyderabad cavalry, and one regiment of Guides cavalry.

Of these twenty-one regiments are armed with lance, sword, and carbine, and nineteen regiments with sword and carbine only.*

Each regiment has a complement of ten British officers, including one medical officer and seventeen native officers.

The paucity of British officers with regiments of the Indian Army has of late years attracted considerable attention. It is contended on the one side that to enable these regiments to meet the troops of European powers on equal terms it is necessary to largely augment the number of the British officers. On the other side it is pointed out that an increase in the number of the British officers means a proportionate decrease in the strength and importance of native officers; and that, apart from other considerations, the service will thereby lose a greater part of its attraction for the best classes of those fighting men who now come forward freely for enlistment. For it must be

* Two or three of these latter, under regimental arrangements, have armed their front rank men with lances.

remembered that ninety-nine per cent. of the native officers have served their time in the ranks, and have worked their way up to their present position. The question appears to hinge on one important point which has not yet been settled. That question is: Are the Indian cavalry intended for use in European warfare, or are they maintained entirely for use in India and on its frontiers?

If it is intended to ask them to take their place in line of battle with British cavalry against the best cavalry nations of Europe, then undoubtedly more British officers are required. If, on the other hand, they are required only for Asiatic warfare and against Asiatic troops, then the present complement of British officers is sufficient. In making such a statement, it is not intended for a moment to cast a slur on the splendid body of native officers who now hold Her Majesty's commission. For it is conceded, and by none more readily than by native officers themselves, that, to obtain the best results, a certain leavening of British officers is indispensable. Let us allow that the present proportion is sufficient, if the reserve of officers were sufficiently strong to keep it permanently at that strength throughout a long campaign. Under present arrangements no such reserve exists, and it might well happen that in a single battle every one of the nine British officers might be killed or wounded. It is to guard against an occurrence of this sort that an augmentation in the number of British officers is advocated.

As far as the actual training of a regiment and its

preparation for such warfare as falls to its lot in India and on its frontiers, the proportion of British officers now allowed perhaps gives better results than would be obtained from employing an augmented number. There is perhaps too great a tendency to look to European models as those on which all success in the future is to be founded. But it is open to question whether sufficient allowance has been made for differences of temperament and characteristics; whether it has been carefully ascertained if methods which produce the best results amongst the soldiers of one nation are likely to be equally successful with those of another; whether the training, formations, and manœuvres imperative for the cavalry of great Powers ever on the verge of war are equally imperative for the Indian cavalry, with a due regard to the work that is before it.

To take one example alone: the German officer, from the day he joins the service to the day he leaves it, spends three-fourths of his existence on parade, in the riding school, or in the lecture-room, in constant contact with his men, for whose training he is personally responsible, and which he himself carries out.

Without for a moment disparaging one nation or the other, it requires very little consideration to see that the British officer has from the earliest times been brought up to a different conception of his duties. Centuries of conquest and a thousand victories have indelibly engrained in the British officer the notion that he is born to lead; that the spirit, the dash, and the enterprise is his; and that to a subordinate rank, that of the non-commissioned officer, is best relegated the minutiæ of the soldier's initial training and education.

The success that has hitherto attended the Indian cavalry is in a great measure due to the maintenance of this principle. The British officer deals with broad questions and larger issues, whilst the native officer and non-commissioned officer are suitably, and to their own satisfaction, employed in the minutiæ of the inner working of squadrons. The tendency during the past decade has undoubtedly been towards Germanising the Indian trooper, and to those who know him, and have had the honour of serving with him, it can hardly be added with satisfactory results.

From this it must not be concluded that the drill, turn-out, and smartness of the Indian cavalry have not been improved. Undoubtedly they have, but in gaining this result it is open to question whether we have not commenced to lay ourselves open to the same grave mistakes which made the Indian light cavalry the laughing-stock of pre-Mutiny days. The Indian trooper has special attributes which fit him in a marked degree for reconnoitring, outposts, foraging, raiding, and rapid operations of every description. He is, in fact, the beau-ideal of a light cavalryman, who is so invaluable to an army in the field. But he is not a heavy dragoon, and it is doubtful whether he will ever make one. Previous attempts show that it is not his *rôle* to pose as a cavalry soldier of the rigid type, to manœuvre in brigade and division for battle-field shock tactics.

At the beginning of this century there was a clearly-defined line between heavy and light cavalry. Heavy cavalry was reserved for actual weight-to-weight charging on the battlefield, whilst the light cavalry performed all such duties as are included in the screening of the army, reconnoitring, and raiding. But nowadays we have abolished this distinction; heavy cavalry, like the Life Guards and Dragoon Guards, weighing from twenty stone to twenty-four stone per trooper, take their turn at screening and reconnoitring duties with the light cavalry, while the light cavalry are expected to take their place in line with the heavy cavalry in battle.

Taking the case of the Indian cavalry as an integral portion of the Imperial cavalry, would it not be wiser to return to this old distinction? As light cavalry, the Indian cavalry would be invaluable in any part of the world. As dragoons they would probably be inferior to most of the cavalry in Europe.

Without entering further into the region of conjecture, it will be more profitable to look into the later campaigns in which cavalry has been used, and from the deductions of the past to endeavour to presage the *rôle* which it will be required to fill, at any rate in India and on its frontiers, in the near future.

In Europe there has been a tendency during the last quarter of this century to decry the value of cavalry. The immense improvement in firearms and artillery has led many writers to declare that the days of cavalry are passed, that it is merely an effete remnant of the days of chivalry, which the first great war will wipe from the face of the earth. But in Asia the comparative supremacy of the arms is different. The only cavalry that exists in Asia worthy of the name are our own cavalry and the Cossacks of the Russian service, and both of these have established so commanding a reputation in Asiatic warfare that the cavalry *moral* is probably higher there than in any part of the world.

And the reason is not far to seek. Both have established a practically unbroken record of success, for not only have they easily defeated any bodies of cavalry that they may have met, but they have on all occasions so severely handled such infantry as they have been called upon to charge as to have secured for the cavalry branch a moral superiority in nearly every campaign.

The Indian cavalry is especially dreaded, for to be charged by these redoubted warriors means loss, and often very severe loss. The decadence of the moral influence of cavalry in Europe is directly due to the small loss which the individual trooper inflicts, even when he charges under the most favourable circumstances, and after getting well home, by surprise, or manœuvre, unharmed by the infantry fire. If we may judge by the past, no such immunity awaits those with whom the Indian trooper gets on hand-to-hand terms. An Indian brigade, launched under the extremely favourable terms with which Bredow's brigade charged the French infantry at Mars-la-Tour, would in all probability have practically wiped the French from the field, instead of inflicting only a loss that might be counted in tens.

It has been suggested that the next great European war will commence with great cavalry battles, that each side will first mobilize its cavalry and send forth a huge screen, which will at the same time cover the mobilization of its own side, whilst it endeavours to pierce the opposing screen. The idea is fascinating, but, however practical in Europe, where distances are comparatively short and forage and supplies comparatively plentiful, such an undertaking would be practically impossible, even if the opportunity occurred, on the frontiers of India. The only formidable body of cavalry in Asia besides our own is the Russian, and at no possible point of contact beyond our borders could the country support one, much less both, of two such formidable opposing forces of horsemen. For it must be remembered that to be effective cavalry movements of this description must be so rapid as to make it quite impossible to supply their wants from depôts in rear. Such a force, therefore, must either live on the country or be tied to work systematically from advanced depôt to advanced depôt, which careful forethought may have formed in the possible theatre of operations.

Putting aside the possibility of the Indian trooper crossing lances with the Cossack, a contingency which the splendid system of defence which has been established at all threatened points, year by year, places more in the background, it will be gathered from past experience that the employment of masses of concentrated cavalry will be practically unknown. It will be noticed that the largest unit which has been actually manœuvred and launched to the charge at any one time in a battle is a regiment, and that more frequently still the attack of individual squadrons has been the most effective use to which cavalry could be put.

Let us first look at the Afghan War of 1878 to 1880, two years during which the cavalry had ample opportunity of showing its value.

CHARGE OF CAVALRY AT DEH SARAK.

At 1 a.m. on the morning of March 24th, 1879, a small mixed force of cavalry, artillery, and infantry, under Brigadier-General Tytler, started to attack the village of Mausam, which lies in the broad valley of the Kabul River, not far from Jellallabad. The force consisted of—

90 lances 11th Bengal Lancers.
60 lances 13th Bengal Lancers.
2 guns 11-9 R.A.
150 bayonets 1st Battalion 5th Fusiliers.
250 bayonets 1st Battalion 17th Foot.
50 bayonets 27th Punjab Infantry.
50 bayonets 2nd Gurkhas.
Total 650 men.

The village of Mausam was situated on high ground, sloping down towards the level bed of the river valley, and was fortified in the usual Afghan manner, with towers and walls of a conglomerate of mud and boulders. Its right lay on a deep nullah, whilst 200 yards from its left flank a lesser nullah ran past it at right-angles. On the further side of this latter nullah was a level plateau.

As the troops approached the position, they reached without opposition a chain of three small villages, which directly faced the village of Mausam, at a distance of only 800 yards. The operation so far had been of the nature of a surprise, but now the Afghans, fully alive to their danger, turned out in great numbers in answer to the call of their tom-toms, and manned the walls and towers, threw out parties in front of the village, and occupied in strength the plateau away to their left. At the same time, a heavy fire was opened on the British troops, not only from the front, but from the chain of small villages which they had just occupied and passed through, and which now lay in their rear. The 17th Foot, the 5th Fusiliers, and the Native Infantry, immediately formed for attack, and the guns opened fire at 750 yards range.

Meanwhile the cavalry, under Captain Thompson, of the 13th Bengal Lancers, and Lieutenant Heath, of the 11th Bengal Lancers, slipped, unobserved, into the shallow nullah which ran into the enemy's position between Mausam and the plateau. The British infantry steadily pushed home its attack, and the 17th Foot, supported by the rest of the infantry, gallantly stormed and captured the key of the position.

The enemy's left flank, posted on the plateau, was so interested in watching this operation, that the cavalry was completely forgotten, until Captain Thompson, using the cover afforded by the nullah with the greatest skill, suddenly burst upon them. The Afghans were at this moment formed up in line four or five deep, and received the cavalry with a volley at fifty yards range. But the surprise was complete, the foot soldiers were too much taken at a disadvantage to take steady aim, and with the loss of two men killed, and six or seven wounded, Captain Thompson and his men were into them. Out of 300 Afghans, fifty were killed; and of the remainder, many were wounded, and the whole body, utterly routed, took refuge in the hills.

THE CAVALRY AT FATTEHABAD.

On April 2nd, 1879, the advanced guard of Sir Sam Browne's column lay at Fattehabad, a village about eighteen miles northwest of Jellallabad on the road to Kabul. This advanced guard consisted of—

2 squadrons 10th Hussars.

2 squadrons Guides Cavalry.

4 guns R.H.A.

400 bayonets 17th Foot.

300 bayonets 27th Punjab Infantry.

300 bayonets 45th Sikhs.

1 company Sappers and Miners, the whole under the command of Brigadier-General Charles Gough.

At about 1 p.m. on that day it was reported by the piquets and vedettes that large bodies of the enemy were advancing from the south-west, the direction of the advance being such as to take directly in flank any further movement of the British force along the road to Kabul.

General Gough immediately got his men under arms and sent out the Guides Cavalry, under Major Wigram Battye, to reconnoitre. Finding that the enemy held steadily on, the General determined to take the initiative rather than await an attack. Leaving, therefore, 300 infantry and two troops of cavalry to protect the camp, he moved out with the rest of his force to the support of the Guides Cavalry, which was now in close contact with the enemy. Pushing on with the cavalry and horse artillery, the General found the enemy to the number of 5,000 posted on the crest of an open stone-strewn plateau, both flanks of which rested on steep inclines which completely commanded the cultivated valleys beneath. The crest of the plateau was strongly fortified with breastworks, the fire from which swept the gentle slope to the enemy's front. The position was about one mile in extent. Whilst awaiting the arrival of the infantry, the cavalry and artillery advanced to within 1,200 yards of the enemy, and opened fire, though apparently with no very great effect, for the enemy, instead of remaining in his position, boldly threw out lines of skirmishers, which commenced advancing on the guns. At once grasping the serious tactical mistake which the enemy were making, General Gough determined to lead them still further astray, by retiring quietly, and drawing them on to the now rapidly approaching infantry. In this manœuvre he was successful. The enemy forsook his position, and issued into the open in dense masses. At this moment the 17th Foot arrived, and forming into line, prepared to charge with the bayonet.

The cavalry now seized its opportunity with great promptitude. Turning on the now thoroughly committed foot soldiers of the enemy the 10th Hussars and Guides Cavalry boldly charged into the heavy masses opposed to them. The direction of the charge of the Guides was towards the enemy's centre, whilst the 10th Hussars, wheeling outwards, attacked those bodies of the enemy who were pressing in and threatening the right flank of the British line. As they started to charge, the Guides came under a heavy fire, and their gallant commander, Major Wigram Battye, as well as the Ressaldar Major, and several of the men, were killed. At this moment, and just as they were closing on the enemy, the Guides came suddenly on a most formidable nullah. To hesitate was to be lost, and not only lost, but to jeopardise the battle, for at such moments, in Asiatic warfare, much hangs on the turn of a die. The occasion found the man, in Lieutenant Walter Hamilton, the young officer on whom the command of the Guides had devolved. He at once jumped boldly into the nullah and followed pell mell by his men, scrambled across it, and, clambering up the opposite bank, fell, in broken formation, but with great fury, on the enemy.

This action of the cavalry was completely decisive,

and killing upwards of 400 of the enemy, scattered them in every direction, the pursuit being carried on for several miles. The Guides numbered only eighty sabres, and the 10th Hussars about the same. The decisive nature of the charge against immensely superior numbers of unbroken and hitherto victorious infantry is therefore particularly instructive.

CAVALRY ACTION NEAR KABUL.

One of the very few occasions on which any body of cavalry larger than a regiment has fought together under one commander, was at Kabul, on December 13th, 1879. But even here, though four regiments were represented, the total force did not exceed eight squadrons, and even these, it will be noticed, were not manœuvred or used as a brigade.

Brigadier-General T. D. Baker's infantry brigade was on this occasion engaged with the Afghans on the Siah Sang hill sides, and thinking that he might have some difficulty in dealing with so many detached parties of the enemy, Sir Frederick Roberts despatched Brigadier-General Massy with his cavalry brigade to his assistance. General Massy accordingly started from Sherpur with one squadron 9th Lancers and two squadrons 14th Bengal Lancers, and marched towards the Siah Sang heights with instructions to drive off 500 Afghan cavalry, who were believed to be about to attack the rear of General Baker's force.

On reaching Siah Sang, General Massy found two squadrons of the Guides Cavalry in the plain to his left, and two squadrons of the 5th Punjab Cavalry on the flat ground to his right; and he was shortly afterwards joined on the heights by the latter, and by another squadron of the 9th Lancers. The total cavalry force on the field, therefore, now consisted of eight and a half squadrons.

The information regarding the enemy's cavalry proved to be incorrect, but General Massy discovered a considerable body of Afghan infantry occupying the southern portion of the Siah Sang range, who opened fire on the cavalry as soon as they appeared. Dismounting a party of the 9th Lancers, he opened fire on the enemy, and seeing that they were inclined to retire, ordered one squadron of the 9th Lancers, supported by two squadrons of the 5th Punjab Cavalry, to follow up, and should an opportunity occur, to charge them.

One squadron 9th Lancers and two squadrons of the 14th Bengal Lancers followed as a reserve.

At the same time the Guides Cavalry in the plain below, working independently, swept round the base of the hills so as to intercept the enemy's retreat. Coming first in contact with the enemy, the Guides charged briskly, and did great execution, and immediately afterwards the squadron of the 9th Lancers, under Captain Butson, charged home, killing a great number of the enemy. Captain Butson, however, fell, shot through the heart, the Sergeant-Major and three men were killed, and two officers and eight men were wounded. The enemy fought most determinedly; and though they were broken and dispersed, and had suffered severe loss, yet many of them, getting cover in ditches and nullahs, kept up a galling fire on the cavalry until they were finally disposed of. The affair was short, sharp, and decisive, and the charges of the 9th Lancers and Guides Cavalry were particularly deserving of commendation.*

THE CAVALRY AT PATKAO, NEAR KABUL.

Information having been received that some 1,000 or 1,500 of the enemy were at Patkao awaiting reinforcements, it was decided to send a small cavalry force to break up the combination.

Accordingly at 3.30 a.m. on the 1st July, 1880, the following troops, under the command of Brigadier-General Palliser, marched for Patkao:—

1st Punjab Cavalry, 226 sabres.
2nd Punjab Cavalry 155 sabres.
19th Bengal Lancers, 183 lances.
Total, 564 with 13 British officers.

The village of Patkao was situated not far from the banks of the Logar River, the intervening ground being cultivated and intersected with water cuts; with a few small-walled villages scattered about amongst the crops. The General's first intention was to have driven his force in between Patkao and the river, thus compelling all fugitives to take to the more open country which led to the Altimur Pass. But the enemy's vedettes evidently gave ample notice of his approach. For when within 2½ miles of Patkao, some horsemen

* Official account.

were seen to the left front evidently observing the brigade. These were shortly joined by a small body of infantry with a standard. In the distance, about four thousand yards off, could be seen the low range of rounded undulating hills which here stretch across the valley, and behind which it was estimated that Patkao was situated.

Changing his original intention, General Palliser altered the direction of the head of the column, and advanced towards the party of the enemy visible, covering his advance with a line of scouts; detaching two patrols of twenty sabres each to protect his flanks as well as to reconnoitre the enemy. The enemy's vedettes and parties disappeared, and the brigade advanced unmolested to the low range above mentioned. On breasting the crest of it, however, Patkao was nowhere visible, but only a succession of rolling underfeatures stretching for upwards of a mile further. Continuing the advance, the village of Patkao at last came in view away to the right front, whilst the enemy, in compact formation but in full retreat, were visible to the left front, moving towards the Altimur Pass. Another body of the enemy about 1,000 strong, mostly infantry, but with a few cavalry, could be seen about two miles off and straight ahead.

General Palliser halted his scouts and reconnoitring patrols, and calling up his main body, took ground to the left, using the ravines and ridges as cover so as to creep up as close to the enemy as possible. But the enemy, fully alive to the danger, was meanwhile making off as fast as possible. A direct pursuit was therefore ordered, 1½ squadrons of the 19th Bengal Lancers, and two squadrons of the 2nd Punjab Cavalry being in the first line, whilst the second line consisted of one squadron 1st Punjab Cavalry and one squadron 2nd Punjab Cavalry. The advanced guard and reconnoitring parties, as they came up with them, joined the first line. Owing to the difficulty of the ground, it was some time before the brigade came in contact with the retreating enemy, who were now much broken and flying either singly or in small parties. The ground here became very stony, broken and in parts precipitous, advantages of which the enemy fully availed himself, each party of Afghans fighting desperately when brought to bay.

The pursuit was continued for a space of two hours, and covered a distance of eight miles beyond Patkao, the men only drawing rein when within a few miles of the Altimur Pass. The supporting squadrons during the pursuit were echeloned behind each flank of the first line, and did great execution amongst those of the enemy who escaped to the right or left of the leading line.

At 9 a.m., having arrived at impassable country, and the horses being a good deal blown, General Palliser sounded the "rally" and collected his squadrons.

The brigade reached camp again at 6.30 p.m., having covered forty miles during the day.

As often occurs in cavalry combats, the question of how to bring off the wounded had to be solved. In civilized warfare it is possible and perfectly humane to leave the wounded in neighbouring villages under care of the villagers, but in fighting fanatics like the Afghans, to leave a wounded man behind is to leave him to certain death by torture. It is, therefore, imperative to bring off the wounded, and this fact alone hampers much the free action and free ranging power of cavalry in these countries. On the present occasion, litters were made with lances and the men's puggris, and villagers were impressed to carry the wounded. One officer and thirty-two men had thus to be carried. The enemy lost heavily, leaving fully 200 dead on the field, and it was only the broken nature of the country which saved them from further loss. The British total loss was one officer, thirty-two men, and thirty-three horses.

A good instance of the great moral effect of the charge of a small body of cavalry is afforded by the action at Khar during the Chitral campaign of 1895. On the occasion referred to, a brigade of infantry was heavily engaged with superior numbers of the enemy; night was coming on, and the tribesmen were advancing with great determination. The only cavalry available was fifty sabres of the Guides Cavalry, under Captain Adams and Lieutenant Baldwin, who were concealed from the enemy's view by a spur. Peering round the extremity of the spur, these officers became aware of the advance of large numbers of the enemy, estimated at 2,000, who were boldly crossing the open to make an enveloping attack on the infantry brigade. Acting with the greatest promptitude and dash, the Guides at once charged, and so sudden was their onslaught, so unexpected was a cavalry attack, that the whole mass of the enemy halted, and then turned and fled, hotly pursued, and severely punished by the horsemen. The effect of this charge was not merely momentary, but established the supremacy of the cavalry arm for the rest of the campaign.

Such are a few of the occasions on which cavalry has been used during the last twenty years. To return to the original point raised, it would appear that the tactical use of cavalry in bodies, larger than a regiment, is improbable in any Asiatic campaign that is likely to fall to the lot of the Indian cavalry, and that, therefore, it would seem advisable for it to aim at maintaining the highest attributes of light cavalry, rather than too strictly to imitate European cavalry, which is trained to fulfil a *rôle* in many essential particulars different.

MOUNTED INFANTRY.

Though the use of mounted infantry, as the term is understood in Europe, is in Indian frontier warfare of very rare occurrence, yet there are countries, such as Burmah, in which mounted infantry has done invaluable service. The necessity for organized mounted infantry, that is to say, of infantry mounted on ponies by companies and regiments, as apart from infantry made mobile for a particular march or operation, by the use of carts, ponies, or pack animals, is usually to be attributed to three causes. These are, the unsuitability of cavalry for the work in hand, *i.e.*, the country being ill-adapted for the *arme blanche*;

the necessity for a rapidly moving force when no cavalry is available; or the climatic unsuitability of the theatre of operations to the cavalry horse.

During the winter of 1879-80, a force of mounted infantry was raised at Kabul, but after a trial of several months the experiment proved a failure, and was abandoned. The chief causes of failure were those common to hastily-raised mounted troops. The men, and in some cases the officers, were quite inexperienced in the feed, keep, and care of horses or ponies; the consequence being that the corps at the date of its disbandment was rapidly becoming a standing hospital of sore backs and sick ponies. On the other hand, there was plenty of good rough-and-ready cavalry at hand, which was more mobile, and quite as efficient in the use of firearms, as the mounted infantry. The *raison d'être* of such a force did not, therefore, exist, and it died a natural death.

But in Burmah, the deadly nature, as far as horses were concerned, of the climate, made it impossible to keep any large number of cavalry regiments in the country, and those that perforce remained lost nearly all their horses. On the other hand, the ample supply of local ponies standing only from about 12 hands in height, but inured to the climate, immediately suggested the advisability of replacing cavalry by mounted infantry.

The nucleus of the force consisted of ninety-four men under Major E. C. Browne, Royal Scots Fusiliers, made up of thirty men Royal Scots Fusiliers, fourteen of the Rangoon Volunteers, and fifty of the Burmese

Police. A little later, some men of the 2nd Hampshire Regiment, having provided their own ponies, volunteered for mounted infantry, and were accepted. This hastily-raised body was mounted on Burmese ponies, and was armed—the British soldiers with artillery carbines and bayonets, and the Burmese with spears and daos; some men also carried revolvers. The saddles were of the English hunting pattern.

Owing to various losses, this small force had by the summer of 1886 dwindled down to forty rifles, and it was then decided to put the corps on a more regular footing, and to increase its numbers.

The work of raising this new corps was entrusted to Lieutenant-Colonel W. P. Symons, of the South Wales Borderers. It consisted of 11 companies, each of 75 rifles commanded by a British officer. Of the 75 rifles, 25 were British soldiers and 50 were native soldiers. The complement of non-commissioned officers in each company was one sergeant, one corporal, two havildars, and two naiks. The officers, non-commissioned officers, and men of each company were drawn as complete units from the different regiments then serving in Burmah. The objection to this system which is usually raised is that the drafting off of picked officers and men to mounted infantry impairs the fighting efficiency of the regiment from which they are drawn. This disadvantage happily did not here exist, for the greater part of the fighting in Burmah had to be done by small detachments, making the employment of a whole regiment rarely necessary.

The whole corps of mounted infantry was mounted on

Burmese ponies at an average cost of about Rs. 100 each. They averaged 12 hands 1¾ inches in height, and had an average girth of 56¾ inches. Their courage and endurance is wonderful, they work without shoes, and live and thrive on unhusked rice, bamboo leaves, and green grass.

Colonel Symons, in raising the corps, impressed on the officers and men under him the fundamental principle of mounted infantry. He laid down that its *raison d'être* was to provide a means of transporting infantry soldiers with greater rapidity and less fatigue to themselves than would be possible if they had to march on foot in an exhausting climate, as well as to enable it to act effectively against an enemy capable of dispersing and retreating faster than our foot soldiers could follow with any hope of coming up with them.

The broad principles laid down for the training of companies were: To accustom the ponies to stand fire; to practice a few simple forms of drill, both mounted and dismounted; route marching; and the loading up and marching with transport animals. Whilst the tactical training was to consist of practice in protecting the front and flanks and rear of a force; the approach to and surrounding of villages; and the art of rapidly and effectively transmitting information. Though none of the officers and men had had any previous experience of mounted infantry work, it was found that in ten days a company could, both as regards ponies and men, be sufficiently trained to take the field. In November of the same year the force was increased from 850 men to 1,600, and the strength of companies was raised from 75 men to 100 men, half being British soldiers and half native.

Each man brought his own rifle and bayonet with him from his regiment. Bandoliers, each to hold fifty rounds, were served out, but, owing to the difficulty of getting the loops exactly to fit the cartridges in a climate by turns hot and cold, wet and dry, it was open to question whether the usual infantry pouches would not have proved equally serviceable.

Various kinds of saddles were tried. Besides the ordinary hunting saddle, a large number of charjama* saddles were issued. These, though cheap, were condemned by all officers as not suitable for the work and liable to give sore backs. Finally, the police saddle, made much on the lines of a cavalry saddle, was found on the whole to be the best.

Various ways of carrying the rifle were tried, but eventually it was concluded that the rifle was best carried in the man's right hand, resting across the front of the saddle.

That the mounted infantry fulfilled its mission in enabling men to cover great distances was repeatedly manifested, and one or two instances may be given as typical examples. Thus, on November 19, 1886, a party of fifty men, under Colonel Symons, were fourteen hours in the saddle and covered forty miles. Again, seventy rifles of the same company, under the same officer, two days later were fifteen hours in the saddle and covered thirty-two miles of road, besides a considerable amount of work in the jungle. In

* A local article made of blanketing.

January, 1887, Captain Golightly, 60th Rifles, rode with a portion of his company for over fifty miles, being seventeen hours in the saddle; these marches being performed, be it remembered, by men who a month or so before had never been on a horse.

MOUNTED INFANTRY SURPRISES IN BURMAH.

During the summer of 1887, Boh Shwe, a very notorious rebel leader, who had long eluded every effort to capture him, was reported to have taken refuge in the Arakan hills, on or near the old frontier of Lower Burmah. In October, certain information of his whereabouts was received by Major Harvey, of the South Wales Borderers. This officer immediately made a forced march of fifty miles with a party of 71 mounted infantrymen, and, discovering the rebel camp, he rushed it at noon on October the 5th, and killed Boh Shwe and ten of his followers. The rest of the gang, 200 in number, were pursued for two miles in dense jungle, and were so thoroughly defeated and dispersed that they never collected again.

Such examples illustrate the legitimate *rôle* of mounted infantry—to take the place of cavalry when none is available, in so far as reconnaissance work is concerned, and to transport foot soldiers distances greater than they could march at a more rapid rate. Should war be again necessary in Burmah, or on its frontiers, the experiences gained with regard to the relative value of cavalry and mounted infantry under the climatic conditions that exist these will be of considerable value.

CHAPTER IX.

ENGINEERS AND PIONEERS.

The engineers of the Indian Army are divided into three corps—the Bengal, Bombay, and Madras Corps of Sappers and Miners, each corps consisting of a certain number of companies. The rank and file of these corps are natives of India; but the officers, and a certain proportion of the non-commissioned officers, are drawn from the Royal Engineers.

In the Pioneers we have a branch of the service which has no exact parallel in other portions of the British Army. A Pioneer battalion is enlisted, drilled and trained as any other native infantry battalion of the line; but in addition, the officers and men are taught the elements of field engineering, in so far as the making of roads, simple bridging, and defensive works are concerned. There are in all seven Pioneer battalions, of which three are stationed in the Punjab, one in Bombay, and three in Madras. The experience which these Pioneer battalions gain is almost perennial, for it is rare for a year to pass without an expedition taking place in one part of the frontier or another, and with these expeditions almost invariably goes a Pioneer battalion. In time of peace the Pioneers perform the ordinary duties of a line regiment, besides keeping up their mechanical training, and occasionally assisting in the construction of public buildings or works, as opportunity may occur.

The value of the Pioneer battalions has been most signally exemplified in every campaign since they were raised. Working in combination with the Sappers and Miners, the very best results have been obtained. The two corps dovetail together in the most business-like manner, for whilst those works, such as permanent bridges, are being constructed by the Sapper and Miner companies, the Pioneers are employed in the making of the roads and other work which does not require the same amount of trained professional skill.

The question has been raised, whether it would not be more suitable to officer the Pioneer battalions with officers of the Royal Engineers, rather than with infantry officers, and a good many arguments can be raised on both sides. The officers of the Pioneer battalions naturally claim the credit of having raised and trained these battalions, and point with natural pride to the excellent work they have done under the existing system. On the other side the argument is intimately connected with a still larger question, the whole matter of the employment of Royal Engineer officers in India. It is manifest that in the Corps of Royal Engineers, as well as in the other departments of the army, a certain establishment of officers must be kept up, in preparation for war, whose services in peace time it is difficult to utilize. In India, employment for these extra officers is with difficulty found in the Military Works Department, and in the purely civil Department of Public Works, and it is now suggested that useful and appropriate employment could be found by handing over the officering of the Pioneer battalions to the Royal Engineers.

Without venturing to express a decided opinion one way or another, and looking at the matter from the broad standpoint of the general good of the army, it is perhaps permissible to point out that a double gain would accrue to Government by the introduction of such a reform. In the first place the extra Royal Engineer officers would be suitably provided for, and suitably employed; and, secondly, fifty-six infantry officers now employed with Pioneer battalions would be released to aid in the scheme now under consideration, for increasing the number of British officers with native regiments, which scheme is hanging fire for want of money alone.

On taking the field the various companies of Sappers and Miners form, as a rule, part of the divisional troops, and work under the orders of the Commanding Royal Engineer, under the direct orders of the General Officer commanding. Amongst the Divisional troops will also be found, as a rule, one or two Pioneer battalions, and these are, from time to time and for specific objects, placed under the control of the Commanding Royal Engineer.

CHAPTER X.

COMMISSARIAT.

When the theatre of war is practically destitute of supplies, as is very generally the case on the frontiers of India, the feeding of an army and its formidable train of pack animals is a work of considerable magnitude, and requires in the heads of the department concerned administrative qualities of the highest order.

It has been very rightly remarked of Indian campaigns that the question of supply occupies more of a general's attention than the movements of the enemy, and that administrative ability of the highest order is required to bring operations of any magnitude, or which extend over any prolonged period of time, to a successful conclusion. With a first-class commissariat officer on his staff an immense load of responsibility is removed from a commander's shoulders, whilst one who is incompetent or indolent may well jeopardise the very existence of the force. To the everlasting credit of the Indian Commissariat, be it recorded, that on no single occasion have the troops, through any fault of the department, failed to receive each man his daily ration. On the other hand, on several signal occasions, the forethought, energy, and administrative ability of commissariat officers have saved bodies of troops, if not from destruction, yet from probable decimation.

Though it may occasionally be necessary for men to be short of food, and to undergo certain hardships during the course of a campaign, and though in a European climate, no great loss may accrue from such deprivations, the case is very different in a tropical climate. Here, unless we are prepared to lose a large percentage of our men, they must be properly fed. Apart from questions of humanity, it is necessary to bear in mind two imperative facts in this connection. The first is that our army is so small that we cannot afford to lose the thousands of men which can disappear without weakening one of the immense modern armies of the European military powers. And secondly, no man fights so well as when he is in good health, well nourished, active, and strong; and this, therefore, for a soldier meeting odds of ten to one, as not infrequently happens, is an absolute essential.

But not only is the Indian commissariat officer heavily handicapped by want of roads, and the necessary use of pack transport to get his supplies to the troops, but the actual packing and preservation under the climatic conditions that exist add to the anxieties and uncertainty of his calculations. It may be laid down as a very general axiom that administrative ability, combined with physical activity, are more conducive to success in Indian warfare than is tactical skill. The enemy's tactics are, as a rule, very simple and easily met, whilst our own tactical movements almost invariably follow the hitherto successful and almost stereotyped manœuvre, which consists of a combined frontal and flank attack. It is evident, therefore, that in the commissariat department should be found some of the ablest officers in the service. But here comes a difficulty which so far has not been successfully met, the difficulty in making the department popular amongst officers. The same difficulty exists in all armies, for the strife of battle is naturally more attactive to the keen soldier, than the useful but unattractive work of supplying food and stores for others to fight upon. The usual devices, such as giving enhanced pay and attractive uniforms, have from time to time been tried, by way of attracting officers, but with indifferent success. It seems probable, therefore, that further advance in the matter of pay will be necessary before a steady flow of young officers into the department can be expected.

The general system on which the Indian commissariat, in common with similar departments in other services, works during the campaign is as follows: At the port of disembarkation, or at the head of the railway, is formed the main base commissariat store. At important points on the lines of communication, and at the front, are formed depôts, varying in size, according to the number and requirements of the troops immediately dependent on them. Such depôts may, in a long line of communication, be from forty to fifty miles apart. Between them, and ten to twelve miles apart, are small intermediate depôts, with sufficient supplies only for the wants of the small detachments which guard the posts along the line of communication. Supplies, after these depôts and posts are established, are moved up as required by a regular post-to-post system of convoys, whilst any extra call for supplies is met by pushing to the front large through convoys, which work independently of the post-to-post service. Some short distance behind the operating force is the advanced depôt, which is pushed on as the troops move forward.

COMMISSARIAT AT KABUL.

It has been mentioned that careful forethought in the matter of supplies has on occasion saved a force from serious loss or perchance complete destruction. One of the best known instances of this was in Kabul, during the mid-winter of 1879-80. Here the military sagacity of the chief commissiariat officer, Captain A. R. Badcock,* working under the orders of Sir Frederick Roberts, foresaw the possibility of great tribal gatherings and hostile combinations interfering with the regular supply of the troops during the winter. And bearing in mind the lesson taught by the entire annihilation of Elphinstone's force forty years before, he took time by the forelock, and quietly, and without attracting attention, gradually accumulated a sufficient reserve of supplies to feed the whole force for three months. The result of this forethought was immediately felt when the British force came to be besieged in Sherpur. The General's mind was freed from all anxiety regarding the feeding of his men. The officers and men, being well fed and nourished, faced the great odds with even courage, and the enemy through their spies learning the comfortable

* Afterwards Quartermaster-General in India.

circumstances under which the besieged were placed, and the length of time their supplies would last, were proportionately discouraged.

Commissariat in Burmah.

The commissariat arrangements during the campaign in Burmah were, of a necessity, different from the arrangements usually made in a frontier expedition. The problem before the troops was the conquest and pacification of a large continent, the work of the Commissariat Department, to feed numberless detachments spread broadcast throughout that area. In the ordinary run of campaigns there are at most two or three lines of communication, and the troops are for fighting purposes more or less concentrated. The work of keeping them supplied with food under these circumstances is considerably simplified. In Europe the rule is for an army to spread for subsistence, and to concentrate only when a battle is imminent. But in countries devoid of supplies no advantage is gained by spreading, but rather disadvantage, for the work of supply is thereby much complicated. In Burmah, however, this problem had to be faced; for the troops had perforce to be scattered as part of the plan of campaign.

The original plan of operations merely aimed at a sudden advance on Mandalay by river and the capture of that place. It was calculated that the capture of the capital would, with so easy-going and unmartial a nation as the Burmans, have a decisive effect; and that the pacification of the country would follow without the necessity of extended military operations. Orders, therefore, were issued for only one month's supply to be arranged for, this being subsequently increased to six weeks' supply, with a reserve of six weeks' more. The campaign and pacification of the country, as events proved, occupied not several weeks, but several years.

As soon as it became apparent that extended operations had become imperative, and flying columns began to move and detached posts to be formed, the strain on the Commissariat Department became very heavy. The staff, in officers, warrant officers, non-commissioned officers, clerks, agents, and menials, had rapidly to be increased by drafts from India, and a great network of supply trains established. These calls on the administrative ability of the Department increased until there were more than one hundred and fifty detached posts in all directions, spread about throughout an enormous tract of country, which had, in addition to the flying columns which were constantly and suddenly on the move, to be supplied with their daily food.

Bakeries had to be established for the supply of fresh bread to all these, and numerous butcheries for the slaughter of cattle for their meat rations.

In some cases where detachments were posted in districts which were impassable during the rains, food had to be stored beforehand to cover four, six, and sometimes even nine months' consumption.

One of the many difficulties in the matter of supply in this, as in other campaigns where mixed forces of

Europeans and natives of India are employed, is attributable to the fact that different rations are required for the different nationalities and even tribes. Thus in Burmah there were fighting side by side British soldiers, Sikhs, Pathans, Gurkhas, Punjabis, Bengal and Bombay sepoys, Madrassis, friendly Burmese, and many other tribes and nationalities. The national food of each of these numerous sects had to be provided for. Apart from questions of caste, which in themselves require careful watching, it is only natural that troops should keep their health better when fed on food that they are accustomed to than when reduced to strange and uncongenial food. Thus the British soldier would become a poor fighting man if reduced for a few weeks to a diet of goat, rice, pulse, and the like; whilst the stalwart Sikh would rapidly sicken if fed on what is to him such foreign food as tinned Australian mutton, bread, cocoa, and the like.

In nearly every post and detachment several of these different elements would be combined, and the work of the Commissariat Department consequently complicated in proportion.

But not only has the Department to contend against the actual difficulties of the situation, but the utmost vigilance has to be exercised in guarding against the dishonesty of contractors and departmental subordinates, both European and native. In Burmah, where close supervision by British officers was practically impossible, a vast field for dishonesty and peculation was opened out, and it is perhaps questionable whether the elaborate system of accounts and checks is in any sensible degree effective in discountenancing this evil.

COMMISSARIAT MIRANZAI EXPEDITION, 1891.

It not infrequently happens that an expedition has to be undertaken at a moment's notice, and in such cases the resources of the Commissariat Department are very highly tried. Thus on April 4th, 1891, some working parties of the 29th Punjab Infantry were attacked whilst road-making on the Samana Range, about forty miles west of Kohat, and a few men were killed. It was decided to at once punish the Miranzai tribe, who were responsible for the outrage, and for this purpose ten battalions of infantry, two regiments (six squadrons) of cavalry, three batteries of artillery, and one sapper company were ordered to mobilize for service. The Commissariat base was formed at Kohat, with an advanced depôt at Hangu, thirty miles in advance, which by April the 8th was in fair working order. On this date three and a half battalions of infantry, two squadrons of cavalry, and four mountain artillery guns were at Darband, thirty-six miles from Kohat, other regiments being pushed on as fast as possible with such carriage as could be raised locally by the civil authorities. A great strain was thus thrown on the small advanced depôt at Hangu. No supplies were procurable locally, and so necessary was it considered to make a show of force as soon as possible at the front, that all carriage collected was first reserved for equipping regiments and field hospitals, and pushing them up as far as Kohat. This left the commissariat stores somewhat in the lurch, and it was necessary to halt some of the troops at Kohat till supplies came up. To ease the strain on the Department, regiments were allowed to purchase in the open market five days' supply; this allowed of the advanced depôt at Hangu being filled up with a small reserve of commissariat stores.

The advance of the force on to the Samana was arranged to take place as soon as the chief commissariat officer could guarantee that the troops would be able to advance from Hangu and Darband with three days' supply in hand, leaving at the same time a reserve of three days' supply at Hangu.

April 17th was fixed as the date for the general advance, and by this date all the commissariat arrangements were complete. Considering the lack of carriage, the suddenness of the call, the scarcity of local supplies, and taking into consideration that the river Indus and upwards of eighty miles of country separated the advanced depôt from the railway head, the performance may be considered a very creditable one.

It will be gathered from the foregoing instances that the Commissariat Department is one of the most important in the service. All that is required is so to raise the solid advantages of the Department as to attract a more ample flow of officers into it.

CHAPTER XI.

Transport.

Soldiers who have never served out of Europe perhaps hardly appreciate the immense difficulties which have to be faced when campaigning in countries where pack animals instead of railways, and coolies instead of carts, have to be used for the porterage of the supplies of an army.

The experiences of the French in Madagascar in 1895 have probably served to emphasize the fact that the only way to carry out a prolonged campaign successfully in a tropical climate, and where pack animals only are available, is on the liberal system which many decades of frontier warfare has taught the Indian army to be indispensable. To attempt European methods, or European economies, in the matter of supply and transport, is to court not only heavy losses from sickness and disease, but as a natural corollary heavy defeat in the field. If the French in Madagascar had been opposed to tribes with even a moiety of the courage and enterprise of the mountain tribes who live on the borders of India, it is doubtful whether a single man would have returned to France to tell the tale. As it was, the French losses from disease alone brought on by attempting European methods in a country unsuited to them, caused a loss estimated at 5,000 men. Apart from questions of humanity, the effect on an army like our own, which is recruited voluntarily, of a loss of that description, would be to paralyze recruiting altogether. Men who join the service voluntarily are ready enough to run the ordinary risks of battle, but they would very naturally refuse to face conditions which tended towards deliberately sacrificing their lives to a false economy. As the French general acknowledged at the end of the campaign, the only way of carrying on a war in a tropical climate, is on the methodical principles and with the immense trains of pack transport which years of frontier warfare has taught the Indian army to be indispensable.

Those who have not had the experience of the French general stand aghast when they notice, for instance, that upwards of 30,000 pack animals were required for the carriage and maintenance of 18,000 men who took part in the relief of Chitral. Yet, here we have two campaigns which were being carried on at about the same time, both successful, but one with practically no loss from disease and the other with an immense loss. There is little doubt that the force which relieved Chitral, working on the principle which has been found indispensable in tropical warfare, would have reached Antananarivo in half the time that it took the French to reach that point, and with merely a nominal loss.

Intimately connected with the question of transport is the number of camp followers which accompany an expedition on the Indian frontiers. For it must be remembered that every follower means an extra mouth to feed, and consequently, in countries like these, which are devoid of supplies, extra pack transport to carry that food. But here again we shall find that experience has taught the Indian army that, though it undoubtedly increases the difficulties of a campaign, it is more conducive to success to reserve the fighting men for fighting work and to delegate the duties of cooks, grooms, servants, etc., to non-combatants. In Europe a force of 10,000 men is by no means a force of 10,000 fighting men, about one-third being occupied in duties unconnected with fighting. On the other hand an Indian division of 10,000 men means a force of 10,000 unhampered fighting men. Nor is the mobility of an Indian force diminished by these seemingly large numbers of followers and pack animals. On the contrary, it is sensibly increased. It will march in a tropical climate at a rate which would leave a force moving on the European system far in the lurch, and will arrive at its destination perfectly fit and ready to fight, instead of in a disorganized, worn-out, and completely inefficient condition.

It has, perhaps, become apparent from former chapters that the successful prosecution of military operations, more especially if they be of a prolonged nature, demands administrative characteristics of the highest quality. Without claiming perfection for it—for few things are not capable of improvement—it may be boldly stated that the Indian pack transport service is the finest and most efficient in the world. Allowing this, and allowing the vital part that it plays in the success of every campaign, it may be conceded that an ample study of this important subject will not be misplaced.

The pack animals used are mules, camels, donkeys, bullocks, and occasionally elephants. Of these a fixed number of mules, camels, and elephants is kept up in peace time, with an establishment in officers and non-commissioned officers, and drivers capable of augmentation in time of war. And here comes in one of the great drawbacks to the maintenance of pack transport, namely the immense expense that has to be incurred in its upkeep during peace time. Carts can be stored at a merely nominal cost, but a pack animal, which carries only 160 lbs. in a campaign, has to be fed every day of his existence in peace time, and not only fed, but kept in such hard condition that he can take the field at a moment's notice.

As in other countries, the great difficulty is to make the transport service popular with British officers. Hundreds of them will volunteer for transport work during a campaign, but it is with the greatest difficulty that officers can be induced to join the department permanently. The chief reason for this is that the commissariat and transport are an amalgamated department, and many officers who would gladly join a transport service will not face what appears to them to be the uninteresting drudgery of a commissariat office. The amalgamation has been made both for economical and administrative reasons which are, no doubt, imperative, but such amalgamation is distinctly detrimental to the popularity and consequent efficiency of the transport service.

This is particularly noticeable at the commencement of a campaign, for at this time the most

experienced departmental officers of the combined de-
supply, and consequently the working of the transport
partment are more urgently engaged in questions of
service falls to the hands of regimental officers who have volunteered for the campaign. It occasionally happens that some of these latter have had previous experience in the field and can at once take their places, and render valuable services, but more often these officers have had no experience beyond marching along the Grand Trunk road in time of peace.

Thus in the Chitral campaign of 1895, owing to the paucity of skilled departmental officers, the charge of the transport of each brigade had to be entrusted to volunteers, some of whom were very young, and wanting in the necessary authority and experience. The weak point in such an arrangement was immediately apparent on the opening day of the campaign. The Malakand Pass was stormed and taken by two Brigades, one of which was detailed to hold the Pass during the night, and the other to return to its bivouac on the south side of it. One very steep single file track was the only road to the summit, and the confusion that necessarily arose, when next day the baggage and supplies of the advanced brigades attempted to get over the pass, may better be imagined than described. Here was a case in point where highly skilled and highly experienced transport officers could alone be expected to contend with such grave difficulties as existed.

In the case of a single track like this the first matter to be settled would be to appoint certain fixed hours for the up traffic and certain fixed hours for the down traffic. This would be done by an officer of the Quartermaster-General's Department, or in his absence by the senior transport officer on the spot, who should undoubtedly assume the responsibility of issuing the necessary orders. Next, a calculation must be made as to the time it takes a pack animal or batch of pack animals to reach the summit, and an estimate made as to the probable number of animals that will be able to start within the prescribed limit of time, for it is manifestly unwise to keep animals standing loaded up for many hours when a simple calculation will show that they cannot possibly ascend that day. Again, in facing an almost precipitous ascent like the Malakand, a continuous string of animals should not be attempted, nor should they be fastened together nose to croup. Yet both of these grave errors were noticeable. In making a steep ascent, pack animals naturally stop to take breath at certain points, generally at a spot where the gradient becomes a little less steep after a severe pull; but if the animals are working in a continuous string, and more especially if they are tied together nose to croup, no such breathing time is possible. Consequently the weaker animals fall exhausted, the whole of those in rear are stopped, some, perhaps, in the very steepest part, and kept standing till they drop, the general result being an absolute block.

To obviate this, the animals should undoubtedly be started in small batches of ten or twelve, with their heads free, and with a good interval between each batch.

At the top and bottom of such a steep ascent, and at intervals up it, should be placed transport officers to regulate the traffic. And at the worst places, and where mules are liable to throw their loads, small fatigue parties should be stationed ready to at once load up and start off any mules which are thus obstructing the road.

As a campaign proceeds, and roads are made and officers gain experience, the transport service drops into a regular and admirably worked organisation, but undoubtedly at the commencement very experienced and able officers are required with the leading brigade.

The peace establishment of pack transport animals is augmented in time of war by purchase and by hire, camels and mules being purchased, whilst donkeys and bullocks, as well as camels and mules, are hired. There are two systems of hire, the one by the month, Government feeding the animal and employing the owner; and the other by results, so to speak, payment being made for so many pounds of stores delivered at such and such a point on the lines of communication; the owner making his own arrangements for the feed of himself and his animals. After considerable experience, it has been decided that this latter system of hire is very much the most satisfactory.

In hiring by the month, it is to the direct interest of the owner that his animal shall do as little work as possible. With the simple guile of the Asiatic, he will therefore manage to give his animal a sore back, or it will, whilst grazing, stray away for weeks at a time, or better still it will die a spurious death, and the owner will receive full value from Government for an animal which, far from being dead, has been spirited away and perhaps sold for a handsome price.

During the Afghan War, when the transport service, as we know it now, was in its infancy, the claims made against Government for loss of hired animals were enormous, and there is little doubt that some of these had been bought twice and sometimes even three times over.

Under the weight delivered system, however, all these evils are avoided. It is to the direct interest of owners to nourish their animals, and to preserve them from sore backs, and the Commissariat Department is partially or wholly relieved of the heavy care of feeding them. The only drawback to the system is its expense. Thus in the Chitral campaign the rate paid was one rupee per regular stage, for every 80-lb. package delivered at its destination. Chitral itself lies at a distance of somewhat over 200 miles from the base store at the railway head. Good stout bullocks might be seen carrying four and even five of these packages, and donkeys two and sometimes three of them. Such a bullock therefore earned Rs. 4 or Rs. 5 each stage and Rs. 85 on the trip, and a donkey Rs. 2 or Rs. 3 and Rs. 34 to Rs. 51 on the trip. Taking the distance at 17 stages, an excellent bullock can be bought outright for Rs. 60, and a very good donkey for Rs. 20; therefore it would appear as if Government were losing enormously over the transaction. As a matter of fact, however, experience has proved that this system is cheaper than the one described above, where the animals are hired by the month.

The general system on which the transport service is worked is as follows:—To each regiment is handed over its allotted proportion of transport animals, generally mules and camels. These are placed under the charge of the regimental transport officer. To each brigade is appointed a brigade transport officer who is responsible for the whole of transport of the brigade, and is attached to the staff of the Brigadier-General. When two or more brigades are in the field a divisional transport officer is appointed who assumes executive charge of all the brigades. In operations which require more than a division a very senior officer, entitled the Director of Transport, is employed.

It will be noticed that during the march from Kabul to Kandahar regiments were made responsible not only for the transport of their own tents and baggage, but also of the supplies which were to feed them on the road. This system is sometimes still further extended during brief operations, or where water transport is used, by making even smaller units responsible for their own stores.

Thus, when an Indian contingent went to Egypt in 1882, each company of infantry or troop of cavalry landed complete, down to its stores and hospital establishment, and could, the moment it landed, take the field.

From a purely transport point of view the smaller the units into which it is split the better does it work, but below a certain point arise difficulties connected with the actual daily issue of rations which preclude the practical working of the scheme. This defect was noticed on the march from Kabul to Kandahar, and again during the relief of Chitral. Supplies calculated to last a certain number of days were issued in bulk to regiments, but owing to the want of weighing machines, skilled issuers, and also partially to unavoidable loss, it was found that such regiments found themselves sometimes completely destitute of food several days before they should have been.

It is, therefore, more usual for regimental baggage animals and ammunition mules only to be placed in regimental charge, whilst all the mules carrying supplies for the brigade remain separate under the immediate orders of the brigade transport officer.

To every three mules or camels is allotted one driver, whose duty it is to clean the animals and their harness, to see to their food and drink, and to lead them on the march. To every half troop of from twenty-five to fifty animals a Duffadar is appointed, and to every troop a Jemadar; whilst in charge of four troops or 200 animals is placed a European warrant or non-commissioned officer.

Besides pack animals for transport, there have been used in various expeditions, carts, coolies, and boats. Carts are, of course, the best and most economical form of transport, but it is not always, or indeed, often possible, to use them. The Government pattern cart is two-wheeled, strongly, but lightly built of wood and iron, with pole draught for two mules or bullocks.

Those drawn by bullocks are calculated to carry 800 lbs., whilst those drawn by mules carry 640 lbs. During prolonged operations where comparatively large bodies of troops are employed, the first advance is made with pack transport, but directly the roads have been made passable, most of the work on the lines of communication is done by carts.

On other occasions, such as at the commencement of the Burmah War and of the Chittagong Expedition, navigable rivers give an opportunity for the employment of boats and steamers; whilst in some districts the impenetrable nature of the forest-covered hills, and climatic conditions, make the use of either pack animals or carts impossible, and resort has to be made to the last and most unsatisfactory form of transport, that is by coolies.

Following the precedent set in other chapters, perhaps a detailed account of the working of the transport service under the different conditions that exist, will best elucidate the matter and afford the student practical, as apart from theoretical, information on the subject.

As typical examples of warfare with pack transport, we will take the Afghan War and the expedition for the relief of Chitral. The Burmah War affords useful experience with regard to water transport and cartage, whilst the various expeditions in the vicinity of Assam furnish examples of the use of coolie transport.

PACK TRANSPORT IN AFGHANISTAN.

The most typical instance of the use of pack

transport, as well as that on which the most reliable information is obtainable, is the march of the force from Kabul to Kandahar in 1880.

The scale of camp equipage and baggage allowed was as follows:

BRITISH OFFICERS.

To every British officer (this allowance to include camp equipage)...............	1 mule.*
To every eight officers for mess............	1 mule.

BRITISH TROOPS.

For kit and camp equipage on account of each soldier (this allowance includes weight of great-coat and waterproof sheet)..................................	30 lbs.†
For each public and private follower......	10 lbs.
Cooking pots, per troop or company.......	240 lbs.
For Quartermaster's stores................	400 lbs.
For entrenching tools, per regiment.......	12 mules.
For carrying arms of sick, per troop or company................................	1 mule.
For armourers', farriers', and saddlers' shops, per cavalry regiment..........	3 mules.

NATIVE CAVALRY.‡

For officers................................	80 lbs.
For armourers, farriers, and saddlers......	3 mules.
For carriage of arms of sick................	1 mule.
Bazaar......................................	1 mule.

NATIVE INFANTRY.

For each native officer, inclusive of camp equipage.............................	30 lbs.

* A mule carries 160 lbs.
† This allowance was slightly increased later.
‡ Native Cavalry supply and keep up their own transport.

For each native soldier, inclusive of camp equipage........................ 20 lbs.
For each follower........................ 10 lbs.
For cooking pots, per company............ 160 lbs.
For cooking pots, per native officer....... 10 lbs.
For cooking pots, mess, British officers... 80 lbs.
For carriage of arms of sick, per company. 1 mule.
Bazaar................................ 1 mule.

The following supplies were carried with the troops:

BRITISH TROOPS
(In Regimental Charge).

Tea, sugar, rum, salt, supply for.......... 30 days.
Preserved meat, supply for............... 2 days.
Bread stuff, supply for.................... 5 days.
Atta for followers, supply for............. 5 days.

NATIVE TROOPS
(In Regimental Charge).

Atta.................................. 5 days.
Dhal and salt.......................... 30 days.
Sheep................................. 10 days.

COMMISSARIAT RESERVE.

Army food.............................. 500 lbs.
Limejuice .... 200 gallons.
Preserved vegetables (all that were available).

Bakeries, butcheries, and other necessary commissariat establishments accompanied the force.

Worked out at these rates, 6,000 pack animals were required for a force of 10,000 men. Of these, about 2,000 were required for the carriage of supplies and stores, whilst 4,000 were required for the carriage of tents, personal baggage, offices, ammunition, and water. The scale here laid down is the lowest safe one for operations which may be prolonged for more than a few days under a tropical sun.

Though some such scale as this is necessary throughout a prolonged campaign, yet it is manifest that in any operations that necessitate the rapid assumption of the initiative, the mobilisation of the force would be very considerably delayed if it had to wait for the concentration of many thousand pack animals drawn from all parts of India. Therefore, at the opening of a campaign it is not unusual for the troops to march without tents and baggage, taking only a great-coat and blanket per man. Thus in opening the Afghan War, the two advanced brigades of the Peshawur Force moved to the storming of Ali-Musjid and the capture of the Khyber Pass with nothing but a great-coat per man, and the ordinary scale of baggage was not brought up till the troops issued into the Jellalabad Valley four or five days later.

In the same way the sudden nature of the call for 15,000 men to advance for the relief of Chitral through a roadless and practically unknown mountainous region, necessitated the use of very lightly equipped troops. A blanket, great-coat, and waterproof sheet were therefore alone allowed to each man until the relief was effected. The ordinary Kabul scale of baggage and tentage was then pushed up for the use of the troops during the remaining five months during which the campaign lasted.

One of the greatest drawbacks to pack transport in

countries destitute of supplies, is afforded by the necessity of sending up grain and often hay for the consumption of the animals. Thus, assuming that the line of communications is 200 miles in length, and that each mule carries 160 lbs. of grain, the daily grain ration of a mule is at least 4 lbs. Even, therefore, if he covers the distance in 16 days going, and 16 days returning, he will eat 128 lbs. out of the 160 lbs. of which his load consists. A camel is more economical, for he carries 320 lbs., and if grazing is obtainable will not eat more than from 64 to 96 lbs. of his load. Donkeys and bullocks in the same way will eat from 40 to 60 per cent. of their loads.

It is apparent, therefore, that the question of the number and description of pack transport animals has to be very carefully regulated, when engaged in supplying a large force at any distance from its base. And infinite care is required so to balance matters that no unnecessary accumulation of pack animals takes place at the front, and yet that every unit is sufficiently mobile to take the offensive at any moment.

It will be found that the most economical system will be, first, to employ carts, both Government and hired, for such parts of the line as have been made fit for wheeled traffic. Secondly, the stages beyond this, if fairly level, could be worked by camels, as combining the greatest carrying power with the least consumption. Lastly, hilly, rough, and stony parts of the line would be worked by mules, ponies, donkeys, and bullocks.

The general system in India is for the transport to work on the stage system. At every twelve miles or so on the line of communications is a post, held by the necessary number of troops, at which is stationed a detachment of transport carts or animals. The transport from each post carries loads on to the next post, drops them there, and returns. To fill up unforeseen deficiencies, or to stock fortified positions, at the front, through-convoys, in addition to the daily post-to-post convoys, are employed.

TRANSPORT IN BURMAH.

At the outbreak of the war in 1885 it was reported by the civil authorities that an ample number of steamers and flats could be hired for the despatch of troops up the river both from Rangoon and Prome. It was further reported that no land transport, except elephants, was then available in Burmah, and a recommendation was made that a corps of coolies should be raised for the work of shipping and transhipping stores and supplies as well as for their carriage on shore. A corps of 3,000 coolies was, therefore, raised.

In so far as the loading and unloading of ships was concerned, this corps proved of much value, but when it came to carrying stores by land the great disadvantage of human porterage was at once apparent. It was found that for any march that lasted for more than five days, a coolie could not carry more than his own food and blanket. He was indeed an encumbrance rather than an aid. The coolie corps was, therefore, relegated to its proper sphere, the loading and unloading of ships, coaling, and the carrying of stores for short distances, and its place taken by a locally raised pack-animal and country-cart service.

Reconstituted on a sounder basis, we find that in May, 1886, the transport service consisted of, firstly, nineteen small steamers belonging to the Irrawaddy Flotilla Company, and secondly, of a pack train consisting of 140 elephants and 2,300 ponies. The steamers themselves were not only loaded with stores, but also towed loaded flats and barges as far as Mandalay.

The number of troops employed was just over 16,000, with 3,700 followers.

It will be noticed at once, how greatly the existence of a navigable river diminishes the difficulties of supply and transport.

In Burmah, a proportion of one pack animal to six fighting men sufficed for all purposes, whereas, as we have noticed, in regions where water transport is not available the requirements of a force sometimes reach so high an average as two pack animals to each fighting man.

During the pacification of Burmah the troops were split up into small detachments, and posted at all important points throughout the country. In a similar way the transport was also split up into thirty-one detachments, a suitable number of animals being detailed for each post. The troops stationed at each

post were thus ready at a moment's notice to take the offensive.

The amount of carriage allowed to each rank was as follows:

British officer, 70 lbs., $\frac{1}{2}$ a pony	Baggage	40 lbs.
	Cooking utensils	10 lbs.
	Stores	20 lbs.
Native officer, 30 lbs., $\frac{1}{6}$th of a pony	Baggage	25 lbs.
	Cooking utensils	5 lbs.
N.C.O. and men (British), 22½ lbs., $\frac{1}{7}$th of a pony	Baggage	20 lbs.
	Cooking utensils	2½ lbs.
N.C.O. and men (natives), 16½ lbs., $\frac{1}{9}$th of a pony	Baggage	15 lbs.
	Cooking utensils	1½ lbs.
Followers, 6 lbs., $\frac{1}{20}$th of a pony	Baggage	5 lbs.
	Cooking utensils	1 lb.

The distribution of the transport did not lend itself to the usual system of employing regimental transport officers. They were, therefore, temporarily abolished, and in their place "post" transport officers were appointed. The European Tran port Staff consisted of one General Transport Officer, three Brigade Transport Officers, and five Warrant and Non-commissioned Officers at the headquarters of the Division and Brigades, whilst 18 officers, and 114 non-commissioned officers and men, worked the different posts.

The change from coolie transport, as at first arranged, to pack transport, and the unexpectedly prolonged nature of the operations threw a very severe strain on the transport staff. Instead of a ready equipped pack transport service, to be merely administered and worked, as is usually the case, the animals had to be purchased, the equipment procured and fitted, and the whole thrown into work hurriedly, with newly recruited attendants entirely ignorant of their duties. Added to this, instead of its being possible to mass the transport by brigades or regiments, this raw material had to be scattered at once in numerous small detachments without trained supervision.

In addition to the pack transport it was necessary to hire carts locally to supply the numerous posts. Burmese carts are reported to have been found very weak, having wooden axletrees, which are constantly breaking; the wheels also are wooden and often oval instead of round. With such material and with the various difficulties, both climatic and physical, which had to be overcome, it is manifest that to maintain a system of convoys to such a network of out-stations as existed was a work requiring great administrative ability. To add to the difficulty of the problem, circumstances were constantly altering owing to the sudden movements of troops ordered out to protect villages or to disperse bands of dacoits.

As was mentioned above, river transport on the lines of communication is usually held to materially assist an expedition by reducing the number of mouths to be fed, but a note made by the Principal Commissariat Officer of the Burmah Field Force is worthy of record. He remarks that, although a splendid river transport would appear to facilitate the movement of stores, it actually does not do so. This is, perhaps, more a question of supply than of transport. In loading up a ship or barge with stores, no doubt a great admixture takes place, and the sorting out of these and disembarking them may, where short stretches of river are used, take more time and be less satisfactory than a train of pack transport where each article, on arrival, comes at once to hand. Again, though steamers may cover the actual distance at a very much quicker rate, yet it must be remembered that a too-rapid flow of stores to the front means congestion at the point of disembarkation, and a steamer may be lying for days and weeks waiting to be unloaded, whilst the pack train is making its march steadily, day by day, and on arrival at once places its stores in the hands of the troops. It is apparent, therefore, that a system of river transport, in so far as the forwarding of supplies is concerned, must be very carefully regulated.*

In the conveyance of troops no such disadvantage is apparent, so long as each unit embarks complete, with its arms, ammunition, baggage, and, if possible, its supplies and land transport, so that it is in a position to at once take the field on landing.

Another good example of the combined use of river and land transport is afforded by the Chin-Lushai Expedition of 1889-90.

The troops, followers, transport animals, stores, and supplies arrived by sea at Chittagong in six steamships.

Here they were transhipped into river steamers and

* All this is a matter of loading the flats or steamers. Where railroads are not available the experience of years shows the value of rivers, from the Danube in 1805 and '9 to the Nile in 1885.—ED.

boats, which conveyed them up the river as far as Demagiri.

From Demagiri onwards, land transport, consisting of elephants, mules, and coolies, was used.

The total distance from the base at Chittagong to the front was 279 miles, which was worked as follows:

(1) From Chittagong to Rangamati, distance by river 70 miles, by three small steamers towing flats, and large country boats.

(2) Rangamati to Pesh-ki-Surra, about 35 miles by river, using dug-out canoes of from 1,600 lbs. to 2,400 lbs. burden, with crews of three men each.

(3) Pesh-ki-Surra to Burkul, distance 2 miles, by land, the river being here unnavigable, was worked at first by bullock carts and later by a light tramway.

(4) Burkul to Demagiri, about 41 miles by river, was worked by dug-out canoes of 1,600 lbs. burden, with crews of three men.

(5) Demagiri to the front, distance 131 miles, was worked by elephants, mules, and coolies.

The fighting strength of the force was 3,380 men, and the transport employed may thus be tabulated:

(*a*) 3 small steamers towing flats and boats.
(*b*) 495 country dug-outs.
(*c*) 3,293 coolies.
(*d*) 2,196 mules.
(*e*) 71 elephants.

From a transport point of view, the constant change necessitated by the form of porterage available, was a very great disadvantage, necessitating severe labour in the transfer of stores from one means of conveyance to another. The chief hitch occurred at the break in the boat service, owing to rapids, between Pesh-ki-Surra and Burkul, a distance of about two miles only. This bit was, as mentioned above, worked at first by bullock carts and coolies, and later by a tram line, but even when this latter, after several months' delay, had been laid, a distance of 300 yards still remained between the landing stage at Pesh-ki-Surra and the head of the tram line. There were 25 cars on this tram line, each capable of carrying 1,600 lbs., but owing to the steep gradients and sharp curves, bullocks could not be used to drag them, and consequently, 500 coolies had to be employed for haulage, as well as to load and unload the trucks. Each car made three trips a day.

The land transport beyond Demagiri was worked on the staging system, but owing to the difficult and mountainous nature of the country, stages were only from seven to eight miles apart. In parts where no suitable stages could be found so close together, the distance was extended to fourteen or fifteen miles, and the mules from these camps met half way, exchanging loads. Through-convoys were also employed to push up extra stores as occasion required.

There was much sickness and great mortality amongst the transport animals and coolies, owing to the unhealthiness of the climate. Thus out of 71 elephants, 33 only survived. Amongst the mules the percentage of sick usually amounted to from 20 to 30 per cent., and 351 died during the expedition. Of the coolie corps, one corps 800 strong was attacked by cholera, became completely demoralised and had to be disbanded; in another corps, 112 coolies died and 1,096 were invalided.

As in other expeditions, it was found that coolies, as a form of army transport, should only be employed as a last resource. The carrying power of a coolie is only 40 lbs., so that in a country devoid of supplies he eats his own load in a few days. The usual composition of each corps of coolies is as follows:

1 British officer.
1 British non-commissioned officer.
1 2nd class transport agent.
10 Sirdars.
20 mates.
500 coolies.
5 sweepers.

These few instances will, perhaps, serve to emphasize not only the great difficulties which attend the use of pack animals for transport, but also the vital necessity for an army situated as is that of India, to have ready and equipped at all points at any rate the nucleus of a thoroughly reliable and efficient transport service.

CHAPTER XII.

MEDICAL.

The medical service has, in recent years, undergone great changes. The purely regimental system has given place to a system which is mainly departmental. But there are serving in India two theoretically distinct bodies of medical officers. Of these, one portion belongs to what is known as the Army Medical Staff, and the other to its purely local equivalent, the Indian Medical Service. The former is composed of those officers who have elected for general service all over the world, including India, and the latter of those who have elected for purely Indian service. But apart from this primary division, the two sister services are in peace time worked on somewhat different lines. Thus the Army Medical Staff remains in peace time a purely departmental corps, whilst the Indian Medical Service, both in peace and war, combines elements of the old regimental system with the modern departmental development.

In time of war, both services work on the same principle. Certain officers of the Army Medical Staff are attached for the campaign to regiments of British cavalry, battalions of British infantry, or batteries of British artillery; whilst officers of the Indian Medical Service accompany their own regiments of the Indian Army. The remaining officers of both services are worked purely departmentally in the base hospital and advanced field hospitals. The general system, then, during a campaign, is for the surgeon or surgeons in charge of each unit to render first aid to the wounded on and in the vicinity of the field of battle. The cases are then passed into the nearest field hospitals, those for Europeans and Natives being distinct. Here such operations as are necessary take place, and they in their turn are then gradually evacuated, as the patients become sufficiently strong to bear the journey to the rear. Along the line of communications, which lie between the base hospital and the most advanced field hospital, are stationed at intervals of from ten to twelve miles sections of other field hospitals, so that the patients are passed back, stage by stage, and at each stage find a hospital ready fitted up for their accommodation. A medical officer, or medical subordinate officer, accompanies each sick convoy, and carries with him such information regarding each patient as will ensure his receiving due attention on arrival. Telegraphic notice also precedes the sick convoy, warning the hospital authorities at the next stage of the diet required to be ready for the more serious cases.

The chief form of ambulance in use in the Indian Army is the "dhooly." This may briefly be described as a comfortable canvas cot, slung on a pole, and carried by four natives, termed dhooly-bearers. The form of conveyance is not economical from a campaigning point of view, for the feed of the bearers swells materially the commissariat difficulties of the operations. But this form of litter is, as a rule, the only one practicable, owing to the absence of roads, and undoubtedly it has, from a humane point of view, many advantages, being the easiest form of porterage which a badly wounded man can have. When nearing the base, and when good roads are available, two-wheeled ambulances, drawn either by mules or bullocks, are used.

The administrative head of the medical service, during a campaign, is termed the Principal Medical Officer. He forms one of the headquarter staff of the force, and through him the General Officer Commanding issues all orders connected with the hospital arrangements and the care of the sick and wounded.

The important question of suitable ambulances for the cavalry has not yet been satisfactorily solved. It is evidently impossible for bearers on foot to keep up with cavalry when it is engaged in making far-reaching reconnaisances, or to carry off the wounded in cavalry skirmishes, which may occur thirty or forty miles from the nearest camp. In Europe the difficulty is solved in a comparatively easy manner. The wounded are left in charge of the nearest villagers until arrangements can be made for removing them. But no such plan is possible amongst the tribes on the frontiers of India, for the moment the force were to retire every wounded man would be tortured to death, or at best killed out of hand. Mule litters and camel litters have been tried, and both are fairly suitable for slightly wounded men, who are yet incapable of riding, but no increased mobility is gained over bearers on foot, for with a wounded man up it would be impossible to push a mule beyond a walk. If a man is strong enough to stand the jolting of a mule or camel moving at a rapid rate, he might as well be riding his own horse.

As has been before mentioned incidentally, though the medical officers in frontier warfare are seldom or never overwhelmed with wounded, as in the case of a modern European battle, yet campaigning in tropical climates begets epidemics of the severest type, and to contend with these tries very highly the administrative, as well as purely professional, attributes of the medical service.

CHAPTER XIII.

SIGNALLING AND TELEGRAPHY.

The invention of visual signalling, and the extension of the use of telegraphs, have materially added to the mobility, efficiency, and comfort of an expeditionary force, the two methods working in combination with each other, and supporting each other when temporary disabilities interfere with the working of either one or the other. Visual signalling is carried on with flags, when the distances are very short, and the weather thick or cloudy, and heliographs are used on all occasions when the sun is out, as it very usually is in an Eastern country; whilst for night-work specially constructed lanterns are employed. It would thus be possible in a friendly country to keep up a long line of communicating-posts both by day and night. In an enemy's country, however, visual signalling has two main disadvantages. The first is that the messages can be read by the enemy, and the second, that the posts, being situated on commanding points, often some distance from camp, are liable to surprise and capture, especially at night.

The telegraphic service here steps in and makes up for the disadvantages under which the sister service suffers. Telegraph stations can be placed in complete security in the midst of the troops, and both night work and day work can be carried on continuously, and without risk. But the telegraph system is liable to two serious drawbacks; the line can very easily be cut at night by the enemy, without fear of detection, and the wires can be tapped unknown to sender and receiver, though in fighting against uncivilized people this latter evil need not be feared. Reciprocating the aid received, the visual signalling service at once takes up the duties of the telegraph department when its line is broken, and fills the breach till the damage is repaired.

But apart from accidents and breaks in the line, the general operations of the two services during a campaign may be described as follows: When the troops start the signallers march with them, whilst the telegraphic department immediately sets to work to lay the line. Under ordinary circumstances, with the delays that the troops are subject to from the nature of the country or opposition of the enemy, the head of the telegraph line will generally manage to keep up within one march of the front. The visual signallers are, therefore, used for communication between the front and the head of the telegraph.

When the first rush of the campaign is over, and the troops have more or less settled down, the telegraph line is completed to all important points, and visual signalling is then generally used only for work between a camp and its piquets, or for minor work between posts.

There is no telegraph corps in the Indian Army, but during peace time all the important telegraph stations are worked by soldier clerks, under the civil officers of the department. When war breaks out the department furnishes civil officers, soldier clerks, line-layers, and plant, at the shortest notice, and puts up and works the line without troubling the military authorities. Indeed, so independent of aid and go-ahead is this department that even when, as at the commencement of the Chitral Campaign, no Government carriage could be supplied, the Superintendent gathered together mules, donkeys, bullocks, in fact, anything that could be bought or hired, and pushed along, keeping almost abreast of the troops.

In the same way, there is no separate corps of signallers in the Indian Army, but each regiment and battery, British and Native, has a proportion of trained men in its ranks. This system is found sufficiently satisfactory for work on the battlefield, and for minor post-to-post work; but to perfect the scheme it would be necessary to have a corps of signallers entirely separate from the regimental signallers, and working under corps officers. Were there no telegraph department, the raising of such a corps would be imperative; as it is, the two services working in conjunction are found sufficient for all the needs of a frontier expedition.

The value of visual signalling, both by heliograph and by flags, has been clearly demonstrated on many battlefields. Thus at Kabul, in 1879-80, when, during the severe fighting that took place, brigades were temporarily separated from each other, and it would have been impossible to establish communication by means of orderlies, messages were flashed over the heads of the enemy from portion to portion of the force, and complete information of each other's intentions and movements was thus kept up.

Again, in storming the Malakand Pass, in 1895, the Divisional Signalling Officer, who was with the Commanding General, was in signalling communication with every brigade, regiment, and battery of the force, and with the head of the telegraph line, fourteen miles in rear.

CHAPTER XIV.

POLITICAL DEPARTMENT.

A very curious and unique relic of bygone days is still maintained on the frontiers of India. This is the recognition of a civil officer, who under the title of "Political Officer" accompanies all military expeditions. Even as late as the Afghan War, this official was not only entirely independent of the General Officer Commanding the field, but on his own responsibility entered into negotiations with the enemy, and corresponded direct with the Foreign Secretary, and through him with the Viceroy, without any reference whatever to the officer responsible for the military operations. Such a system very naturally proved to be not only unworkable, but highly prejudicial to the successful working out of a campaign. Since the Afghan War, reforms have been instituted, which have, in some measure, mitigated the evil, but a remnant of it still remains. Thus several civil political officers invariably accompany military expeditions, but instead of being entirely independent of the General Officer Commanding, they are now under his orders to a certain extent, and correspond through him. Yet remnants of the evil in minor matters still remain, and it is possible whilst the General and the troops are undergoing the rigours of a compaign, and bivouacking without tents, for a young political officer to be living in the lap of luxury, in a spacious marquee. The system, of which this is but a petty example, is radically wrong, and should undoubtedly be swept away. The real duties performed by the Political Officer are in fact those which should fall to the lot of the Intelligence Department. If, on occasion, it is not possible for the Intelligence Department to produce a military officer with sufficient knowledge of the language and customs of the enemy, it is quite open to employ a civil officer for the work; but it should be clearly and unmistakably laid down, that whilst so employed such civil officer belongs to the Intelligence Department, and is in all ways on exactly the same basis as a military officer in similar employ. Under the present system, the Intelligence Department is placed in an entirely false position, for though this department supplies, before the campaign commences, maps of the proposed theatre of operations, and such information as it possesses regarding the country and its people, yet directly the campaign commences, the General Officer Commanding turns for all his information not to the Intelligence Officer, but to the Political Officer, for the simple reason that the latter is a local expert, whilst the former has often no special knowledge of the particular region. If the title and present semi-civil functions of the Political Officer were abolished, we should arrive at a practical and sensible solution of the case. The Senior Intelligence Officer, whether civil or military, would be General's right-hand man, with regard to all dealings with the enemy, and the collection of information regarding him, and all possibility of friction between the civil and military element would be removed.

INDEX.